THE AUSTRALIAN
Women's Weekly

HEALTHY
EATING

THE AUSTRALIAN
Women's Weekly

HEALTHY EATING

BALANCED, NOURISHING
EVERYDAY RECIPES

Project Editor Siobhán O'Connor
Project Designer Alison Shackleton
Editors Kiron Gill, Megan Lea
Jacket Designer Alison Donovan
Jackets Coordinator Jasmin Lennie
Production Editor David Almond
Production Controller Denitsa Kenanska
Managing Editor Dawn Henderson
Managing Art Editor Alison Donovan
Art Director Maxine Pedliham
Publishing Director Katie Cowan

First published in Great Britain in 2022
by Dorling Kindersley Limited
DK, One Embassy Gardens, 8 Viaduct Gardens, London, SW11 7BW

The authorized representative in the EEA is Dorling Kindersley
Verlag GmbH. Arnulfstr. 124, 80636 Munich, Germany

Copyright © 2022 Dorling Kindersley Limited
A Penguin Random House Company
10 9 8 7 6 5 4 3 2 1
001–326303–Mar/2022

A CIP catalogue record for this book is available from the British Library.
ISBN: 978-0-2415-3146-4

Printed and bound in China

For the curious
www.dk.com

This book was made with Forest Stewardship Council ™ certified paper –
one small step in DK's commitment to a sustainable future.
For more information go to **www.dk.com/our-green-pledge**

Contents

Healthy

What we choose to fuel our bodies with affects not only our weight, but also our entire wellbeing. A good diet can be transformative: it can make us feel mentally alert and helps our bodies to function more efficiently. Critically, it protects us from the onset of chronic disease.

A holistic approach

Taking charge of our eating and cooking from scratch is often a good option for our wallets. Doing so should be viewed in a holistic way – think of it as savings banked to our health account that may work to cost us less in healthcare in the future.

A hectic life can mean that time is enemy number one when it comes to our food choices, often derailing us into making less nutritious ones. What we should be eating should be simple – right? Ironically, it is the constant barrage of mixed health information that can work in reverse, confusing us and making us lose sight of what normal eating is.

As scientists gain more insight into the unique properties of the foods we eat and how these fuel our bodies' nutritional needs and protect us against disease, nutritional guidelines provided by accredited dietary practitioners and government bodies shift in line with these new findings. What never changes, however, is the requirement to eat as many foods that are as close to nature as possible to nourish your body.

In the modern world where diets seem to be all about weight loss, it's easy to forget that we all need to eat really well to optimally nourish our bodies, boost vitality, and give us the best chance of great health – now and into the future.

Nature's wholefood powerhouse

Rather than turning to supplements (although these have their place), you are almost always better to consume the foods that provide these nutrients. In part this is because nature provides a wonderful balance and package of nutrients not found in individual supplements. In addition, plant foods provide a wealth of phytochemicals – substances such as antioxidants that benefit us enormously, way beyond our basic needs for vitamins and minerals.

There are particular foods that are the star players in providing nutrients and phytochemicals. These foods might be high in one particular nutrient, such as shellfish for their outstanding zinc content. Alternatively, a food may have a high level of a phytonutrient known to be beneficial in protecting against a particular disease.

Tomatoes are a good example because they provide a rich source of lycopene, shown to reduce the risk of prostate cancer in men. Other foods boast an army of protective phytochemicals and nutrients: nuts are nutritional powerhouses providing many nutrients including fibre, folate, magnesium, vitamin E, riboflavin, calcium, and protein, along with a collection of different antioxidants. Extra virgin olive oil contains not just healthy, stable monounsaturated fat, but also vitamin E, at least 29 polyphenols (known to be protective in the body), a chemical called squalene that plays a role in protecting your skin from the sun, and a compound called oleocanthal that is anti-inflammatory. Foods such as these all have something extra to offer us.

The best news is that nutritious food does not have to be expensive or exotic. While there are certainly some really interesting foods that are imported from other areas of the world, including berries such as acai and goji, there are even more foods produced locally and available in your local grocer, fishmonger, butcher, or supermarket. Locally grown berries, broccoli, cabbage, watercress, Asian greens, mushrooms, seeds, oats, salmon, mussels, lean meats, and plain yogurt are just a few of the standout foods we can all work more easily into our weekly menus. Look for budget-friendly hero foods too; canned salmon or mackerel, frozen berries, canned legumes, and packets of whole grains all help to make the family weekly budget go further.

How we fill our plates is also important. Your plate should be half-filled with colourful vegetables. Add to this a moderate amount of lean animal protein (eggs, chicken, beef, lamb, pork, or fish) and/or a plant-based one (tofu, tempeh, beans, and legumes), and a wholegrain carbohydrate (brown rice, barley, quinoa, and pastas made from pulses). While fats should make up a smaller part of our diet, they nonetheless have a key role to play in our health. Replace hydrogenated oils and saturated fats with moderate amounts of beneficial ones from nuts, seeds, olive oil, fatty fish, and avocados.

Taking the path towards better health

This book is designed to help all of us get more wholefoods on our plate to nutrient-boost our diets. When you and your family eat well, you'll feel more energetic, you'll radiate better health, and you'll give your body the best protection you can against lifestyle-related diseases. Healthy food is attainable for everyone, via simple recipes created using an abundance of supermarket-sourced wholefoods. In our mix are plenty of recipes that take 30 minutes or less; for winter months, there are recipes with brief preparation times that need a little longer to work their magic in the oven. Also included are wholesome recipes for entertaining or feeding a crowd, where you may want to make several dishes to share.

Above all we hope this book will inspire you to broaden the array of foods that you and your family consume, all put together in the most delicious but completely doable way.

Healthy eating has never tasted so good!

LIGHT
BITES

Whether you are looking for a quick, satisfying lunch or inspiration for a light supper, you will find it here – all the benefits of wholefoods without sacrificing flavour.

Chicken and egg salad with yogurt green goddess dressing

HIGH-PROTEIN | PREP + COOK TIME **25 MINUTES** | SERVES **4**

PER SERVING | Energy 855kcals | Carbohydrate 12g of which sugar 8g | Fat 57g of which saturates 16g | Salt 0.9g plus seasoning | Fibre 10g

The good fats in avocado give the vibrant green dressing used here a very luxurious texture and creamy taste. Try it on another occasion with chargrilled meats, fish, or vegetables, or make it with half the amount of yogurt as a delicious dip.

4 skinless boneless chicken breasts (800g)

2 garlic cloves, halved

4 eggs, at room temperature

200g mixed baby heirloom tomatoes, halved

1/2 cup (15g) firmly packed mint leaves

300g celery sticks, thinly sliced

2 tbsp extra virgin olive oil

2 baby cos lettuce (260g), torn

1 1/2 large avocados (480g), sliced

1/3 cup (25g) flaked natural almonds, toasted

salt and freshly ground black pepper

green goddess dressing

75g baby spinach leaves

1 1/2 cups (75g) firmly packed chopped mint leaves

1/2 large avocado (160g)

1 1/4 cups (350g) Greek-style yogurt

1 tbsp lemon juice

1 To make the green goddess dressing, process the spinach and mint leaves until finely chopped. Add the avocado, yogurt, and lemon juice; pulse until smooth. Season with salt and pepper to taste. Refrigerate until needed.

2 Fill a medium saucepan three-quarters full of cold water. Add the chicken and garlic, and bring to the boil. Reduce the heat to low; cook for 10 minutes or until the chicken is cooked through. Using a pair of tongs, transfer the chicken to a plate; set aside to cool. Discard the garlic.

3 Return the water in the saucepan to the boil. Add the eggs; cook for 6 minutes for soft-boiled. Drain and refresh the eggs under cold running water. Peel the eggs, then cut in half.

4 Meanwhile, put the tomatoes and half of the mint leaves in a large bowl; using a fork, crush the tomatoes slightly to release the juices. Add the celery and olive oil; toss to combine. Season with salt and pepper to taste.

5 Shred the poached chicken; divide the chicken, lettuce, tomato mixture, avocado and eggs evenly among 4 serving bowls. Drizzle with the tomato juices, and top each serving with some of the green goddess dressing. Serve scattered with the toasted almonds and remaining mint leaves.

Japanese-style tofu salad

VEGETARIAN | PREP + COOK TIME **30 MINUTES** | SERVES **4**
PER SERVING | Energy kcals 685 | Carbohydrate 72g of which sugar 9g | Fat 29g of which saturates 5g | Salt 2.7g plus seasoning | Fibre 9g

Silken tofu is produced without separating and pressing the soy curds, which results in
a more delicate texture than other forms of tofu, so take care when cutting and coating it
to preserve the shape. It also varies from soft to extra firm; firm silken tofu is used here.

500g firm silken tofu, drained

500g microwave or instant brown and wild rice

1 cup (150g) frozen shelled edamame

50g pea tendrils or shoots

170g fresh asparagus, trimmed,
thinly sliced lengthways

4 spring onions, thinly sliced

1/4 cup (70g) pink pickled ginger, shredded

1/2 cup (90g) brown rice flour

sunflower oil for shallow-frying

2 nori sheets (5g), finely shredded

1 tbsp sesame seeds, toasted

salt and freshly ground white pepper

soy dressing

1/4 cup (60ml) light soy sauce

2 tbsp mirin

1 tbsp extra virgin olive oil

1 tbsp lime juice

1 Drain the tofu, and gently press between sheets of kitchen paper to remove as much moisture as possible. Set aside.

2 To make the soy dressing, put the ingredients in a screw-top jar with a tight-fitting lid; shake well to combine.

3 Heat the rice according to the packet directions. Put the edamame in a large heatproof bowl; cover with boiling water. Allow to stand until thawed. Drain; refresh under cold running water, then return to the bowl. Add the rice, pea tendrils, asparagus, spring onions, and pickled ginger with the dressing; toss well to combine.

4 Cut the drained tofu into 3cm pieces. Place in a large bowl with the rice flour; season with salt and white pepper to taste. Gently turn to coat, taking care not to break up the tofu.

5 Heat enough sunflower oil to come to a depth of 2cm in a deep frying pan over a medium heat; shallow-fry the tofu for 2 minutes on each side or until golden. Remove with a slotted spoon; drain on kitchen paper.

6 Divide the salad among 4 serving bowls; serve topped with the fried tofu, nori, and toasted sesame seeds.

TIP

Mirin, a slightly sweet Japanese rice wine, is often paired with soy sauce in Japanese cooking. It is found in everything from marinades to ramen.

Steamed eggs with chilli sauce

HIGH-PROTEIN | PREP + COOK TIME **55 MINUTES** | SERVES **4**

PER SERVING | Energy kcals 508 | Carbohydrate 24g of which sugar 9g | Fat 38g of which saturates 5g | Salt 2.6g | Fibre 2g

Eggs provide very high quality protein, with a near-perfect balance of the amino acids the human body needs. Scientific research is unequivocal in its support of higher protein diets for weight control, and eggs are a terrific food to boost the protein content of a meal.

8 x 16cm small rice paper rounds

extra virgin olive oil cooking spray

a little rice bran oil

8 eggs

2 tsp sesame oil

150g baby spinach leaves

60g snow peas (mangetout), shredded

2 tsp black and white sesame seeds, toasted

1 cup (25g) Thai basil leaves

chilli sauce

1/3 cup (80ml) rice bran oil

6 long red chillies, thinly sliced

1 1/2 tbsp tamarind paste

1 1/2 tbsp fish sauce

1 1/2 tbsp grated dark palm sugar

1 tbsp light soy sauce

1 tbsp extra virgin olive oil

2 tsp tahini

1 tsp light soft brown sugar

1 To make the chilli sauce, heat the rice bran oil in a small saucepan over a medium heat; cook the chilli, stirring occasionally, for 3 minutes or until soft. Remove from the heat; stir in the remaining ingredients, and mix well to combine. Set aside to cool.

2 Meanwhile, make the rice paper crisps. Spray 1 rice paper round with a little of the olive oil; microwave on high (100%) for 50 seconds or until puffed up and white. Repeat with the remaining rice papers. Set aside.

3 Place a larger bamboo steamer over a large wok of boiling water. Grease four 1 1/2–cup (375ml) ceramic dishes or rice bowls with a little rice bran oil. Crack 2 eggs into each bowl. Carefully place the bowls in the steamer; steam, covered, for 5–8 minutes until the whites of the eggs are set but the yolks remain runny. (The cooking time of the eggs will vary depending on the depth of the bowls.)

4 Meanwhile, heat the sesame oil in a frying pan over a medium heat; cook the spinach, stirring, for 2 minutes or until wilted. Remove the spinach from the pan; combine with the snow peas and 1 tablespoon water, and toss for 1 minute or until bright green.

5 Top the eggs with the wilted spinach, snow peas, sesame seeds, basil leaves, and chilli sauce. Serve with the rice paper crisps.

TIP

The heat of chillies varies. If you'd like a milder sauce, seed half of the chillies before slicing.

Double broccoli pizza

HIGH-FIBRE | PREP + COOK TIME **1 HOUR** | SERVES **4**

PER SERVING | Energy kcals 377 | Carbohydrate 12g of which sugar 8g | Fat 21g of which saturates 9g | Salt 1.2g plus seasoning | Fibre 14g

Broccoli is a part of the *Brassica* genus, which is noted for its high vitamin A, C, and E folate and potassium content. What makes brassicas special, however, is a group of antioxidants called flavonoids. These act as anti-cancer agents and ramp up detoxifying enzyme systems.

1kg broccoli, trimmed, cut into florets

¼ cup (30g) grated Cheddar

1 egg, lightly beaten

¼ cup (40g) finely grated Parmesan

½ cup (130g) bottled passata

350g broccolini (Tenderstem broccoli), trimmed

2 tbsp extra virgin olive oil

100g buffalo mozzarella, torn

½ cup (60g) pitted Sicilian green olives, halved

salt and freshly ground black pepper

1 Preheat the oven to 200°C (180°C fan/400°F/Gas 6). Line 2 baking trays with baking parchment.

2 Process the broccoli florets until finely chopped. Transfer to a microwave-safe bowl, and cover with cling film; microwave on HIGH (100%) for 12 minutes or until tender. Drain, then allow to cool slightly. Put the broccoli in the centre of a clean tea towel; gather the ends of the towel together, then squeeze out as much liquid as possible.

3 Combine the broccoli, Cheddar, egg, and ¼ cup of the Parmesan in a bowl; season with salt and pepper to taste. Divide the mixture evenly between the prepared trays, pressing into two 22cm ovals.

4 Bake the pizza bases for 25 minutes or until golden. Spread each base with the passata, leaving a 2cm border around the edge. Top with the broccolini, cutting any thick stems in half lengthways. Drizzle with the olive oil, and bake for a further 10 minutes.

5 Top the pizza with the mozzarella and green olives. Bake for a further 10 minutes or until the cheese is melted and the broccoli tender. Serve scattered with the remaining Parmesan.

TIPS

- When trimming florets, don't discard the broccoli stems. Save them for another recipe such as the nori crunch salad on page 21.
- If you want to make this recipe vegetarian, replace the Parmesan with a Parmesan-style vegetarian hard cheese.

Farmers' market bowl

VEGETARIAN | PREP + COOK TIME **35 MINUTES** | SERVES **4**
PER SERVING | Energy kcals 480 | Carbohydrate 29g of which sugar 17g | Fat 28g of which saturates 12g | Salt 1.2g plus seasoning | Fibre 11g

Brussels sprouts contain several powerful flavonoids; they also contain large amounts
of vitamin K, a vitamin thought to prevent or at least delay onset of Alzheimer's disease.
Buckwheat, which is similar to quinoa, is a good source of fibre and complex carbohydrates.

400g Brussels sprouts, trimmed, cut into 1cm slices

400g mixed heirloom baby carrots, trimmed, halved lengthways

400g small yellow pattypan squash

2 tbsp extra virgin olive oil

125g kale, leaves coarsely torn

1/4 cup (45g) raw buckwheat

2 tsp tamari

4 eggs

salt and freshly ground black pepper

instant harissa labneh

2 cups (560g) Greek-style yogurt

1/2 cup (105g) drained chargrilled peppers in oil

2 tsp harissa paste

1 tbsp red wine vinegar

TIPS

• Leftover yogurt whey can be saved for up to
2 days to use in smoothies or Bircher muesli,
or to add to a soup.

• You can use chopped tamari roasted almonds
or a purchased mix of toasted seeds, if you like,
instead of the roasted buckwheat.

1   To make the instant harissa labneh, line a sieve with muslin or cheesecloth; place it over a large jug or bowl. Put the yogurt in the lined sieve; season with salt and pepper to taste. Gather the muslin, forming the yogurt into a ball by twisting the cloth. Continue gently twisting until 3/4 cup (180ml) of liquid (whey) has drained from the yogurt into the jug and a firm ball of labneh is obtained (reserve the whey; see tip). Process or blend the chargrilled peppers with the harissa, vinegar, and 1 tablespoon of the whey until smooth. Stir one-quarter of the harissa mixture through the labneh in large swirls. Set aside both the labneh and the remaining harissa mixture.

2   Preheat the oven to 220°C (200°C fan/425°F/Gas 7). Line 2 baking trays with baking parchment.

3   Arrange the Brussels sprouts, carrots, and pattypan squash in 3 rows on one of the baking trays. Drizzle with 1 tablespoon of the olive oil; season with salt and pepper to taste. Roast for 20 minutes or until the vegetables are just tender and starting to brown around the edges.

4   Place the kale on one side of the remaining tray; drizzle with 2 teaspoons of the olive oil, and toss to combine. Put the buckwheat on the other side of the tray; drizzle with the tamari, and stir to combine. Bake at the same time as the vegetables for 8 minutes or until the buckwheat is dry and the kale is crisp.

5   Meanwhile, heat the remaining 2 teaspoons olive oil in a large, non-stick frying pan over a high heat. Crack the eggs into the pan, one at a time; cook for 2 minutes or until the whites are set, edges are crisp, and yolks are cooked to your liking.

6   Spread the instant harissa labneh over the bottom of 4 shallow serving bowls. Divide the vegetables and eggs evenly among the bowls. Sprinkle with the tamari buckwheat. Serve with the remaining harissa mixture.

Japanese oat and nori crunch salad

VEGETARIAN | PREP **30 MINUTES** | SERVES **4**

PER SERVING | Energy kcals 530 | Carbohydrate 17g of which sugar 8g | Fat 43g of which saturates 7g | Salt 0.5g plus seasoning | Fibre 12g

For a portable salad lunch, pack the nori crunch and miso dressing into separate small containers and the salad into a larger one to transport. Assemble the salad just before eating, for maximum crunch and zing.

1–2 small carrots, julienned

1 beetroot, peeled, julienned

stalks of 1 head of broccoli, trimmed, peeled, julienned (reserve florets for another use)

1 cup (50g) coarsely chopped mint leaves

4 cups (160g) baby kale

2 large avocados (640g)

1/2 cup (80g) blanched almonds, toasted

nori crunch

1 tbsp sesame oil

2 garlic cloves, crushed

1 tbsp white miso (shiro miso)

2 nori sheets (5g)

2 tbsp pumpkin seeds, finely chopped

1/4 cup (25g) rolled oats

1/2 cup (20g) firmly packed coarsely chopped baby kale

salt and freshly ground black pepper

miso dressing

2 tbsp white miso (shiro miso)

2 tsp sesame oil

1/4 cup (60ml) apple cider vinegar

1 large garlic clove, crushed

1 tsp pure maple syrup

TIP

You will need 300g julienned vegetables for the rainbow slaw. For the right flavour balance, make sure you have more carrot/beetroot than broccoli.

1 To make the nori crunch, preheat the oven to 160°C (140°C fan/325°F/ Gas 3). Line a large baking tray with baking parchment. Combine the sesame oil, garlic, white miso, and 1 tablespoon water in a large bowl. Finely tear the nori into the bowl. Next, add the pumpkin seeds, oats, and chopped kale; toss well to combine. Season with salt and pepper to taste. Spread the mixture over the prepared tray; bake for 20 minutes or until golden, turning halfway during the cooking time. Set aside to cool on the tray.

2 To make the miso dressing, put the ingredients and 1 tablespoon water in a screw-top jar with a tight-fitting lid; shake well to combine. Season with salt and pepper to taste.

3 To make the rainbow slaw, put the carrots, beetroot, broccoli stalks, and mint in a large bowl. Add a third of the miso dressing, and toss to combine. Divide evenly among 4 serving bowls. Combine the baby kale with another third of the dressing; divide among the serving bowls. Halve the avocados; discard the stones. Add an avocado half to each serving, then drizzle each avocado half with the remaining miso dressing. Serve the salad scattered with the nori crunch and toasted almonds.

Chicken and brown rice larb cups

FAST | PREP + COOK TIME **20 MINUTES** | SERVES **4**

PER SERVING | Energy kcals 446 | Carbohydrate 41g of which sugar 3g | Fat 14g of which saturates 3g | Salt 2.5g | Fibre 4g

Larb is a tangy salad of minced chicken (or pork) and fresh herbs, originating from Laos, but also found in northern Thailand. This version keeps the traditional flavours and instead mixes them with brown and wild rice for extra fibre.

500g microwave or instant brown and wild rice

1 tbsp extra virgin olive oil

500g minced chicken

4 spring onions, thinly sliced

1/3 cup (10g) finely chopped coriander leaves and stems, plus extra leaves, to serve

2 garlic cloves, crushed

2 tsp grated fresh root ginger

2 tbsp fish sauce

2 tbsp lime juice

4 makrut lime leaves, finely shredded

2 baby cos lettuce (360g), leaves separated

1/3 cup (50g) roasted unsalted cashews, chopped

1 cucumber (130g), seeded, finely chopped

1 long red chilli, thinly sliced lengthways

lime wedges, to serve

1 Heat the rice according to the packet directions.

2 Meanwhile, heat the olive oil in a large wok over a high heat; stir-fry the chicken for 4 minutes, breaking up any lumps. Add the spring onions, chopped coriander, garlic, ginger, and rice; stir-fry for 1 minute or until combined. Next, add the fish sauce, lime juice, and makrut lime leaves; continue stir-frying until just combined.

3 Divide the chicken mixture among the lettuce leaves. Top with the roasted cashews, cucumber, chilli, and extra coriander leaves. Serve with the lime wedges for squeezing over.

Chargrilled sides

These flavour-packed sides are stars in their own right, turning the notion of worthy but dull vegetable accompaniments on its head. Quick chargrilling helps to preserve nutrients and colour, and each dish can be used to expand a meal into a more substantial offering.

Hoisin aubergine

PREP + COOK TIME **20 MINUTES** | SERVES **4**

Preheat a ridged cast-iron grill pan over a high heat. Cut 3 aubergines (1.3kg in total) into 5mm rounds on a slight diagonal. Brush the aubergine slices with 1 cup (250ml) hoisin sauce, then spray with extra virgin olive oil. Cook the aubergine, in batches, for 4 minutes on each side or until tender and grill marks appear. Arrange the aubergine slices on a platter. For the dressing, whisk together $1/2$ cup tamari, 2 tablespoons light soft brown sugar, and 1 teaspoon sesame oil; drizzle over the aubergine. Sprinkle with 2 teaspoons toasted sesame seeds, 2 tablespoons fried shallots, and 1 finely sliced long red chilli.

Sweet pepper salad

PREP + COOK TIME **30 MINUTES** | SERVES **4**

Preheat a ridged cast-iron grill pan over a high heat. Cut 2 red onions (340g) into wedges, then spray with extra virgin olive oil; chargrill for 1 minute on each side or until slightly softened. Place on a serving platter. Halve and seed 350g baby sweet peppers, spray with extra virgin olive oil and chargrill for $1^1/2$ minutes on each side or until just tender. Add to the platter with 250g cherry tomatoes, halved. Combine 2 tablespoons extra virgin olive oil with $1^1/2$ tablespoons lemon juice; drizzle over the vegetables. Sprinkle with $1/3$ cup (50g) toasted pine nuts and 220g cherry bocconcini (fresh mozzarella pearls), torn in half.

Courgette and dukkah

PREP + COOK TIME **20 MINUTES** | SERVES **4**

Cut 6 small yellow courgettes lengthways into four. Toss in a large bowl with 2 tablespoons extra virgin olive oil. Heat a ridged cast-iron grill pan over a medium heat; cook the courgettes, in two batches, for 3 minutes on each side or until grill marks appear. Toss the courgettes with 1 teaspoon honey and 2 tablespoons dukkah to coat. Split 1 wholemeal pitta bread in half. Spray with extra virgin olive oil; chargrill for 1 minute on each side until crisp. Serve the bread crumbled over the courgettes with 60g crumbled feta.

Lemony chilli asparagus

PREP + COOK TIME **20 MINUTES** | SERVES **4**

Preheat a ridged cast-iron grill pan over a high heat. Trim 2cm from the ends of 480g asparagus. Group the asparagus spears in threes, side by side, then thread 2 toothpicks or metal skewers through each group to hold them together. Brush the asparagus with 2 tablespoons chilli-infused olive oil. Chargrill for 2 minutes on each side until tender. Serve with baby rocket leaves, finely grated Parmesan, and lemon wedges for squeezing over.

Thai-style fried rice

FAST | PREP + COOK TIME **35 MINUTES** | SERVES **4**

PER SERVING | Energy kcals 432 | Carbohydrate 40g of which sugar 5g | Fat 14g of which saturates 3g | Salt 3.5g | Fibre 3g

You can make this fried rice with chicken by substituting the prawns with 250g shredded cooked skinless boneless chicken breast. If you want to cook your own rice, you will need to do this the night before, spreading out the cooked rice on a tray in the refrigerator to air-dry.

500g microwave or instant brown, red, and wild rice mix

2 tbsp extra virgin olive oil

4 eggs, lightly beaten

4 shallots (100g), thinly sliced

2 tbsp Thai red curry paste

2 garlic cloves, crushed

500g uncooked prawns, shelled, deveined, tails intact

150g mixed Asian mushrooms such as oyster and shiitake

1 red pepper (200g), thinly sliced

2 tbsp light soy sauce

1 tbsp fish sauce

1 tbsp lime juice

1 cup (25g) Thai basil leaves

lime cheeks, to serve (optional)

1 Heat the rice according to the packet directions.

2 Meanwhile, heat 1 tablespoon of the olive oil in a large, non-stick wok over a high heat. Add the beaten eggs, swirling the pan slightly to create an omelette about 20cm in diameter. Using a spatula, pull the egg inwards from the edge of the wok towards the centre to create folds, letting the uncooked egg mixture fill any gaps. Cook for 3 minutes or until set. Still using the spatula, roll up the omelette in the wok, then slide carefully onto a board; cut into 1cm thick slices. Set aside.

3 Heat the remaining 1 tablespoon olive oil in the same wok over a high heat; stir-fry the shallots for 3 minutes or until softened. Add the curry paste and garlic; stir-fry for 30 seconds until fragrant.

4 Add the prawns, mushrooms, and red pepper; stir-fry for 4 minutes or until cooked through.

5 Add the rice and cooked egg; stir-fry for 1 minute until heated through. Stir through the soy and fish sauces, lime juice, and basil leaves. Serve with lime cheeks for squeezing over, if you like.

Roasted broccolini, edamame, and chilli tempeh salad

FAST | PREP + COOK TIME **25 MINUTES** | SERVES **4**

PER SERVING | Energy kcals 416 | Carbohydrate 21g of which sugar 9g | Fat 21g of which saturates 3g | Salt 1.1g plus seasoning | Fibre 12g

The chemical responsible for the heat of a spicy chilli is capsaicin. This fiery little compound has many potential health benefits for the body. It also increases the body's production of heat and can help to clear nasal congestion, making it a great winter food.

300g chickpea tempeh

1 tbsp tamari

1 tbsp runny honey

2 long red chillies, chopped

350g broccolini (Tenderstem broccoli), trimmed

2 cups (300g) frozen shelled edamame

2 tbsp groundnut oil

240g mixed salad leaves

salt and freshly ground black pepper

lime halves, to serve

cashew dressing

2 tbsp cashew butter

1^1/$_2$ tbsp lime juice

1 tbsp tamari

1 tbsp groundnut oil

1　Preheat the oven to 200°C (180°C fan/400°F/Gas 6). Line 2 large baking trays with baking parchment.

2　Using your hands, gently crumble the tempeh into a bowl, forming a mixture of large and small chunks. Add the tamari, honey, and half of the chopped chillies; toss gently to combine. Spread the mixture over one of the prepared trays.

3　Put the broccolini and edamame on the remaining tray; drizzle with the groundnut oil, then toss the vegetables to coat with the oil. Season with salt and pepper to taste. Roast in the oven for 15 minutes or until the broccolini is just tender and the tempeh is golden.

4　Meanwhile, to make the cashew dressing, whisk together the ingredients with 1 tablespoon cold water in a small bowl until smooth. Add an extra tablespoon of cold water if needed to thin.

5　Arrange the roasted broccolini, edamame, and salad leaves in a large bowl; toss gently. Divide evenly among 4 serving plates. Top with the tempeh, and drizzle with the cashew dressing. Scatter over the remaining chilli. Serve with lime halves for squeezing over.

Bang bang salmon salad

HIGH-PROTEIN | PREP + COOK TIME **30 MINUTES** | SERVES **4**

PER SERVING | Energy kcals 539 | Carbohydrate 16g of which sugar 7g | Fat 37g of which saturates 7g | Salt 0.8g | Fibre 6g

Salmon takes the place of chicken in this version of the classic Sichuan street food, with its fiery dressing characteristic of the regional Chinese cuisine. If you don't have a microwave, serve the salmon with steamed brown rice or quinoa instead of the rice paper crisps.

1 tbsp extra virgin olive oil

2 x 250g skinless salmon fillets

2 carrots (240g), julienned

2 midi or salad cucumbers (260g), seeded, julienned

50g pea shoots

4 spring onions, thinly sliced lengthways

1 cup (30g) coriander leaves

4 large rice paper rounds (40g)

extra virgin olive oil cooking spray

2 tbsp sesame seeds, toasted

lime wedges, to serve (optional)

bang bang dressing

1 tsp Sichuan peppercorns

1/2 tsp dried chilli flakes

1/4 cup (45g) sesame seeds

2 tbsp Chinese black vinegar

1 tbsp light soy sauce

1 tbsp extra virgin olive oil

2 tsp tahini

1 tsp light soft brown sugar

1 Heat the olive oil in a large frying pan over a high heat. Cook the salmon for 4 minutes; turn and cook on the other side for a further 2 minutes or until just cooked but still pink in the centre. Set aside.

2 Gently toss the carrots, cucumbers, pea shoots, spring onions, and coriander leaves in a large bowl.

3 To make the bang bang dressing, stir the Sichuan peppercorns, chilli flakes, and sesame seeds in a small frying pan over a medium heat for 2 minutes or until the seeds are golden; be careful not to scorch. Allow to cool, then grind to a fine powder using a spice mill or a mortar and pestle. Put in a screw-top jar with a tight-fitting lid. Add the remaining dressing ingredients; shake well to combine.

4 Spray 1 rice paper round with a little of the extra virgin olive oil cooking spray; microwave on HIGH (100%) for 50 seconds or until puffed up and white. Repeat with the remaining rice papers.

5 Using a fork, flake the salmon into large pieces. Put in a bowl with the bang bang dressing; toss gently to coat the salmon with the dressing. Arrange the carrot mixture on a platter; top with the salmon.

6 Scatter the bang bang salmon with the toasted sesame seeds. Serve with the rice paper crisps and lime wedges for squeezing over, if you like.

TIP

You can shred the carrot with a julienne peeler, mandolin, or V-slicer. If you don't have any of these, coarsely grate the carrot instead.

Couscous and haloumi salad with smoky tomato dressing

FAST | PREP **25 MINUTES** | SERVES **4**

PER SERVING | Energy kcals 590 | Carbohydrate 58g of which sugar 10g | Fat 24g of which saturates 12g | Salt 2.5g plus seasoning | Fibre 15g

The carbohydrates in pulses are absorbed very slowly, giving pulses low glycaemic index values. For example, chickpeas have a GI of 36 (low-GI foods are those with a score of less than or equal to 55) – this makes them very good at filling you up.

1 cup (200g) wholegrain giant couscous (mograbieh)

400g can chickpeas, drained, rinsed

2 courgettes (240g), julienned

200g mixed cherry tomatoes, halved

2 tsp extra virgin olive oil

250g haloumi, cut into 2cm pieces

¼ cup (30g) dukkah

½ cup (15g) coriander leaves, to serve

smoky tomato dressing

1 tbsp extra virgin olive oil

200g mixed cherry tomatoes, quartered

1 small red onion (100g), finely chopped

280g bottled piquillo peppers (pimiento pequillo), drained, finely chopped

1 tsp smoked paprika

¼ cup (60ml) red wine vinegar

salt and freshly ground black pepper

1 To make the smoky tomato dressing, heat the olive oil in a medium non-stick frying pan over a medium heat. Cook the tomatoes, onion, peppers, and paprika, stirring, for 4 minutes or until the tomatoes start to release their juices. Stir in the vinegar. Remove from the heat; season with salt and pepper to taste. Set aside to cool.

2 Cook the couscous in a medium saucepan of salted boiling water over a high heat for 6 minutes or until tender; drain. Put the couscous in a large bowl with the chickpeas, courgettes, tomatoes, and the smoky tomato dressing.

3 Heat the olive oil in a large non-stick frying pan over a high heat. Cook the haloumi for 2 minutes on each side or until golden. Add the dukkah, and toss to coat the haloumi.

4 Add the haloumi to the salad; toss gently to mix through. Serve with the coriander scattered over the top.

TIP

You can slice the courgettes with a julienne peeler, mandolin, or V-slicer. If you don't have one, coarsely grate the courgettes instead.

Loaded avocados with bulgur wheat

FAST | PREP + COOK TIME **15 MINUTES + STANDING** | SERVES **4**
PER SERVING | Energy kcals 642 | Carbohydrate 19g of which sugar 3g | Fat 54g of which saturates 16g | Salt 0.6g plus seasoning | Fibre 9g

Wholegrain bulgur wheat, used for centuries in Middle Eastern cuisine, is high in fibre and has a high manganese content. An essential nutrient, manganese aids calcium absorption in our bodies. It is also vital for normal nerve and brain function.

1/2 cup (80g) coarse bulgur wheat

2 large avocados (640g)

3 spring onions, coarsely chopped

1/2 cup (15g) small basil leaves

220g bocconcini (mozzarella balls), torn

125g heirloom cherry tomatoes, halved

salt and freshly ground black pepper

lemony dressing

1/4 cup (60ml) extra virgin olive oil

2 tbsp lemon juice

1 garlic clove, crushed

1 Put the bulgur wheat in a medium bowl; cover with boiling water. Allow to stand for 10 minutes or until the grains are swollen and tender. Drain well and set aside.

2 To make the lemony dressing, put the dressing ingredients in a screw-top jar with a tight-fitting lid; shake well to combine. Season with salt and pepper to taste.

3 Halve the avocados and remove the stones. Using a dessertspoon, scoop out large chunks from the flesh of the avocado, reserving the avocado shells with the skin intact.

4 Put the soaked bulgur wheat, scooped avocado, spring onions, basil, bocconcini, and tomatoes in a large bowl. Drizzle over the lemony dressing; season with salt and pepper to taste. Mix through gently. Spoon the bulgur mixture into the avocado shells. Serve immediately.

TIP

You could use 1/2 cup (100g) wholegrain couscous instead of the bulgur wheat. Put the couscous in a small heatproof bowl; cover with 1/2 cup (125ml) boiling water. Cover the bowl tightly with cling film. Allow to stand for 5 minutes, then fluff the couscous grains with a fork.

Green quinoa and chicken salad

PORTABLE | PREP + COOK TIME **40 MINUTES + REFRIGERATION** | SERVES **4**

PER SERVING | Energy kcals 651 | Carbohydrate 31g of which sugar 6g | Fat 42g of which saturates 7g | Salt 0.3g plus seasoning | Fibre 8g

Although quinoa is cooked and eaten as a grain alternative, it is in fact a seed. While it might be relatively new to the store cupboard for many of us, quinoa has been a staple food for thousands of years in the Andean region of South America. The Incas reportedly considered it sacred, calling it the 'mother of all grains'.

2 x 200g skinless boneless chicken breasts

4 garlic cloves, thinly sliced

1/2 cup (125ml) extra virgin olive oil

3 tsp finely grated lemon zest

1/2 cup (125ml) lemon juice

1/4 cup (7g) oregano leaves

120g baby spinach leaves

1 cup (200g) white quinoa

1 large avocado (320g)

200g heirloom cherry tomatoes, halved

1 cucumber (130g), thinly sliced lengthways into ribbons

salt and freshly ground black pepper

1 Cut each chicken breast in half horizontally to make 4 thinner fillets. Place in a glass or stainless-steel bowl with the garlic.

2 Whisk together the olive oil, lemon zest and juice, and oregano in a jug. Pour 1/4 cup of the dressing over the chicken; turn to coat well. Cover and refrigerate for 20 minutes.

3 Meanwhile, process the remaining dressing with 40g of the spinach leaves until smooth. Season with salt and pepper to taste. Set aside.

4 Put the quinoa in a fine sieve; rinse under cold running water until the water runs clear. Tip the drained quinoa into a medium saucepan. Add 2 cups (500ml) water; bring to the boil. Cook, covered, for 15 minutes. Remove from the heat; allow to stand, covered, for 5 minutes. Fluff the grains with a fork.

5 Meanwhile, heat a ridged cast-iron grill pan over a high heat; cook the chicken for 5 minutes on each side, or until cooked through and grill marks appear. Allow to rest, loosely covered with foil, for 5 minutes, then cut on a diagonal into 2cm thick slices.

6 Cut the avocado in half; remove the stone. Scoop out the flesh from the avocado using a spoon. Put the quinoa in a large bowl with the spinach dressing; toss to combine. Season with salt and pepper to taste. Add the remaining spinach, avocado, tomatoes, and cucumber; toss through. Serve the salad topped with the sliced chicken.

Supergreens Spanish omelette

HIGH-PROTEIN | PREP + COOK TIME **55 MINUTES + STANDING** | SERVES **4**

PER SERVING | Energy kcals 429 | Carbohydrate 23g of which sugar 2g | Fat 24g of which saturates 7g | Salt 0.8g plus seasoning | Fibre 4g

Leafy greens are without doubt one of the top foods to include in your daily diet. They are among the most nutrient-dense foods, yet contain very few kilojoules and they're anti-inflammatory. Curly kale definitely falls into this category. Not only is it a great source of vitamin C, but it contains phytonutrients that help to support eye health as well.

440g potatoes, cut into 2cm cubes

2 tbsp extra virgin olive oil

1 tsp smoked paprika

3 cups (105g) shredded curly kale

10 eggs

extra virgin olive oil cooking spray

$^1/_2$ cup (60g) frozen garden peas, thawed

$^1/_2$ cup (50g) grated pecorino or Parmesan

salt and freshly ground black pepper

1 Preheat the oven to 180°C (160°C fan/350°F/Gas 4). Line a large baking tray with baking parchment.

2 Toss the potatoes with half of the olive oil and the paprika on the prepared tray; season with salt and pepper to taste. Put the kale in a medium bowl; drizzle with the remaining oil. Using your fingertips, massage the oil into the kale to coat.

3 Bake the potato mixture for 15 minutes; add the kale to the tray, reserving the bowl. Bake for a further 10 minutes or until the potato is tender.

4 Lightly whisk the eggs in the reserved bowl; season with salt and pepper to taste. Spray a 26cm (18cm base measurement) non-stick ovenproof frying pan with the extra virgin olive oil cooking spray. Heat the frying pan over a medium heat. Scatter the potato mixture and the peas over the bottom of the pan. Pour over the egg mixture; cook for 2 minutes or until the egg is starting to set and pull away at the edge of the pan. Transfer the omelette, still in the pan, to the oven; cook for 15 minutes or until the egg is just set in the centre.

5 Leave the omelette to cool slightly before removing from the pan. Scatter the pecorino over the top, and cut into wedges to serve.

TIPS

- Refrigerate any leftovers for easy school or workday lunches, or chop as 'croutons' to toss through a salad.
- Try a bunch of chopped fresh asparagus instead of the garden peas. Parmesan, feta, ricotta, or aged Cheddar can all be used instead of the pecorino, if you like.

Jalapeño steak and watermelon salad

HIGH-PROTEIN | PREP + COOK TIME **25 MINUTES** | SERVES **4**

PER SERVING | Energy kcals 614 | Carbohydrate 89g of which sugar 82g | Fat 25g of which saturates 5g | Salt 0.5g plus seasoning | Fibre 7g

Red meat is rich in zinc, a mineral often typically low in diets. Zinc is essential for immune function; hence you'll find it added to cold and flu remedies. Eating red meat a few times a week is all you need to significantly zinc-boost your diet.

500g beef flank (bavette) steaks or flat iron steaks

2 tbsp pickled sliced jalapeños, plus $^1/_3$ cup (80ml) pickling liquid

2 tbsp extra virgin olive oil

1 large avocado (320g)

1 iceberg lettuce (500g), cut into 10 wedges

1$^1/_2$ cups (45g) firmly packed mint leaves

1 tbsp lime juice

1kg seedless watermelon, rind removed, thinly sliced

1 tbsp black and white sesame seeds, toasted

salt and freshly ground black pepper

lime wedges, to serve

1 Put the steak in a bowl with half of the jalapeño pickling liquid and 1 tablespoon of the oil, making sure the steaks are coated in the liquid. Season well with salt and a good grinding of pepper. Allow to stand for 10 minutes.

2 Meanwhile, process half of the avocado, 1 lettuce wedge, $^1/_2$ cup (15g) of the mint leaves, lime juice, remaining 1 tablespoon pickling liquid, and remaining 1 tablespoon olive oil until smooth. Season with salt and pepper to taste. Set aside.

3 Heat a ridged cast-iron grill pan or barbecue to a high heat. Cook the steaks for 3 minutes on one side or until grill marks appear; turn and cook for a further 3 minutes for medium rare or until cooked to your liking. Allow to rest for 5 minutes, loosely covered with foil.

4 Spread three-quarters of the avocado dressing over the bottom of a large, shallow platter; top with the remaining lettuce and mint, as well as the watermelon. Thinly slice the steak and arrange on the salad; scatter with the jalapeños, and sprinkle over the toasted sesame seeds. Lastly, top with the remaining avocado, cut into wedges. Serve accompanied by the rest of the dressing and lime wedges for squeezing over.

Thai salmon and chia fishcakes with watercress salad

HIGH-PROTEIN | PREP **20 MINUTES** | SERVES **4**

PER SERVING | Energy kcals 606 | Carbohydrate 6g of which sugar 2g | Fat 42g of which saturates 7g | Salt 1.6g plus seasoning | Fibre 7g

Salmon fishcakes can be a great way to ensure dietary intake of omega-3 fatty acids, which are essential for brain health. Chia seeds also contain omega-3 and bump up the content here. In these fishcakes, the fragrant Thai flavours of ginger, coriander, and lime shine.

$1/4$ cup (40g) black chia seeds

1 tbsp grated fresh root ginger

$1/4$ cup (10g) finely chopped coriander leaves and stems

1 shallot, finely chopped

2 tsp finely grated lime zest

2 tsp fish sauce

800g skinless salmon fillets, cut into 2cm pieces

2 tbsp extra virgin olive oil

salt and freshly ground black pepper

watercress salad

1 cucumber (130g), thinly sliced into ribbons

350g watercress, washed, trimmed

1 cup (30g) coriander leaves

1 shallot, halved, thinly sliced

1 tsp grated fresh root ginger

1 long green chilli, finely chopped

2 tbsp lime juice

2 tsp fish sauce

1 tbsp extra virgin olive oil

1 Stir together the chia seeds and $1/2$ cup (125ml) warm water in a small bowl. Allow to stand for 5 minutes to soak.

2 Process the ginger, coriander leaves and stems, shallot, lime zest, fish sauce, and soaked chia seeds until just chopped. Add the salmon; pulse until combined. Season well with salt and a good grinding of pepper.

3 Divide the mixture into twelve $1/3$-cup portions. Flatten into 8cm rounds. Place on a baking tray lined with baking parchment; refrigerate for 20 minutes to firm slightly.

4 Meanwhile, to make the watercress salad, put the cucumber, watercress, and coriander leaves in a large bowl; toss through. Put the shallot, ginger, chilli, lime juice, fish sauce, and olive oil in a screw-top jar with a tight-fitting lid; shake well. Drizzle half of the dressing over the salad, and toss to mix evenly; reserve the remaining dressing to serve.

5 Heat half of the olive oil in a large non-stick frying pan over a high heat. Cook half of the fishcakes for 2 minutes on each side or until browned and cooked through. Transfer to a tray; cover to keep warm. Repeat with the remaining oil and fishcakes.

6 Divide the watercress salad evenly among 4 serving plates. Add 3 fishcakes to each serving alongside the salad. Drizzle the remaining dressing over the fish. Serve immediately.

Lemony chicken and kale broth

HIGH-PROTEIN | PREP + COOK TIME **40 MINUTES** | SERVES **4**

PER SERVING | Energy kcals 438 | Carbohydrate 44g of which sugar 4g | Fat 11g of which saturates 2g | Salt 0.8g | Fibre 5g

Chicken provides more iron and zinc in the leg and thigh meat, which is why thigh fillets are used in this broth instead of breast meat. They are also more flavourful. Plus you'll benefit from a boost of B group vitamins, with niacin as the star player. Lemons and lemon juice contain a range of phytochemicals, including flavonoids.

2 tbsp extra virgin olive oil

4 spring onions, sliced, green ends reserved

2 garlic cloves, sliced

600g chicken thigh fillets, cut into thirds

12 baby new potatoes (480g), halved

1 litre (4 cups) vegetable stock

4 slices of sourdough bread (200g)

1 large courgette (150g), spiralized (see tip)

¼ bunch of kale (65g), trimmed

¾ cup (35g) shredded mint leaves

2 tbsp lemon juice

1   Heat 1 tablespoon of the olive oil in a large, heavy-based saucepan over a medium heat. Cook the sliced spring onions and the garlic, stirring, for 2 minutes or until softened.

2   Add the chicken; cook, stirring occasionally, for 2 minutes, or until the chicken has turned white on the outside. Add the potatoes, stock, and 1 cup (250ml) water; bring to the boil. Reduce the heat to low and cook, covered, for 20 minutes, or until the potatoes are just tender and the chicken is cooked through.

3   Meanwhile, preheat a ridged cast-iron grill pan to a high heat; grill the bread slices for 1 minute on each side or until grill marks appear. Set aside to keep warm.

4   Remove the lid from the broth, and add the courgette and kale. Cook, uncovered, for 1 minute until the kale is bright green. Remove the pan from the heat, then stir through three-quarters of the shredded mint and the lemon juice.

5   Divide the hot broth among 4 serving bowls. Thinly slice the reserved spring onion ends; top the soup with the spring onion and the remaining shredded mint. Drizzle each serving with a little of the remaining olive oil. Serve immediately with the toast.

TIP

Use a spiralizer to spiralize the courgette. If you don't have one, you can shred the courgette using a julienne peeler, mandolin, or V-slicer.

Salmon, broad bean, and labneh omelette

HIGH-PROTEIN | PREP + COOK TIME **20 MINUTES** | SERVES **4**

PER SERVING | Energy kcals 568 | Carbohydrate 9g of which sugar 4g | Fat 40g of which saturates 10g | Salt 1.4g plus seasoning | Fibre 7g

Eggs, salmon, and broad beans combine here to make a high-protein low-carb meal that is not only filling, but tasty as well. Broad beans are rich in plant and soluble fibre, as well as containing manganese, folate, and other B vitamins. You could also use crumbled feta or goat's cheese instead of the labneh, if you like.

8 eggs

1 lemon (140g)

1/3 cup (80ml) extra virgin olive oil

2 cups (300g) frozen broad beans, blanched, peeled

1 cup (25g) fresh dill leaves

4 spring onions, thinly sliced

300g hot-smoked salmon, skin removed, flaked

150g labneh (see tip)

salt and freshly ground black pepper

lemon wedges, to serve

1 Lightly whisk the eggs with 2 tablespoons cold tap water in a large bowl until combined. Season with salt and pepper to taste.

2 Using a zesting tool, remove 1 tablespoon zest from the lemon (alternatively, finely grate the zest from the lemon). Squeeze the juice from the lemon; you will need 1 tablespoon juice. Whisk together the lemon zest, juice and 2 tablespoons of the olive oil in a large bowl; season with salt and pepper to taste. Add the broad beans, dill leaves, spring onions and salmon; toss gently to combine.

3 Heat 2 teaspoons of the olive oil in a heavy-based non-stick frying pan (with a 14cm base measurement) over a medium heat. Add one-quarter of the egg mixture; using a spatula, pull the egg inwards from the edge of the pan towards the centre to create folds, letting the uncooked egg mixture fill any gaps. Cook for 2 minutes, or until done to your liking. Slide the omelette carefully onto a plate; fold over. Repeat three times with the remaining oil and the egg mixture to make 4 omelettes in total.

4 Place the omelettes on 4 serving plates; top each one with some of the broad bean salad and labneh. Season with salt and pepper to taste. Serve with lemon wedges for squeezing over.

TIP

Labneh is a thick, creamy-textured yogurt that has been drained of all its whey. If you would like to make your own, stir 1 teaspoon sea salt flakes into 500g Greek-style yogurt. Spoon into a sieve lined with muslin or cheesecloth; place the sieve over a bowl, gather the cloth, and tie tightly into a ball. Refrigerate for 24 hours until thick.

Indian scrambled eggs

HIGH-PROTEIN | PREP + COOK TIME **25 MINUTES** | SERVES **4**

PER SERVING | Energy kcals 460 | Carbohydrate 37g of which sugar 8g | Fat 24g of which saturates 9g | Salt 1g plus seasoning | Fibre 5g

It's hard to eat poorly when you have a carton of eggs on hand in the fridge, even if there's little else around. Eggs represent compact packets of protein and nutrients ready to be turned into a nutritious meal in minutes.

1/2 cup (40g) shredded coconut

2 tbsp extra virgin olive oil

2 long red chillies, thinly sliced

1/4 cup (25g) fresh root ginger, peeled, shredded

1 red onion (170g), thinly sliced

1/2 tsp garam masala

400g cherry tomatoes, halved

8 eggs

1/2 cup (125ml) canned light coconut milk

2 limes (130g)

1/2 cup (15g) coriander leaves

8 Mountain Bread or other very thin wholegrain flatbreads (200g), warmed

salt and freshly ground black pepper

1 Put the shredded coconut in a small heatproof bowl; pour over 1 cup (250ml) boiling water. Set aside until needed.

2 Heat 1 tablespoon of the olive oil in a large non-stick frying pan over a high heat. Add the chillies, ginger, red onion, and garam masala; cook, stirring, for 4 minutes, or until the onion softens. Next, add the tomatoes; cook, stirring occasionally, for a further 5 minutes until softened. Transfer to a bowl; cover to keep warm.

3 Meanwhile, whisk together the eggs and coconut milk until just combined. Season with salt and pepper to taste.

4 Heat the remaining olive oil in the cleaned pan over a medium heat. Pour the egg mixture into the pan; cook, tilting the pan, until the egg mixture is almost set. Gently stir for 3 minutes, using a rubber spatula, or until the egg is just cooked.

5 Drain the soaked shredded coconut; return to the bowl. Finely grate the zest from 1 of the limes into the bowl; squeeze the juice from the lime (you will need 2 tablespoons of juice). Add the lime juice to the bowl; stir to combine. Cut the remaining lime into wedges.

6 Top the eggs with the warm tomato mixture, coconut mixture, and coriander leaves. Serve with the flatbread and lime wedges for squeezing over.

TIP

Mountain Bread is baked using a traditional family recipe for a unique type of flatbread that has been made in the mountains of Lebanon for thousands of years. If you can't find it, look for a similar thin, wholegrain flatbread such as markook, lavash, or rumali roti (handkerchief bread).

Lentil, pear, and fennel salad with goat's cheese

FAST | PREP + COOK TIME **30 MINUTES** | SERVES **4**

PER SERVING | Energy kcals 677 | Carbohydrate 41g of which sugar 18g | Fat 42g of which saturates 11g | Salt 1.9g plus seasoning | Fibre 15g

Pulses are packed with different types of fibre and a type of carbohydrate called resistant starch that is especially important for gut health. The friendly bacteria living in your colon thrive on resistant starch, and it is the product of this fermentation process that boosts our gut health and overall immune function.

1 cup (200g) puy or other green lentils

1/3 cup (80ml) extra virgin olive oil

1/4 cup (15g) coarsely chopped flat-leaf parsley

2 Beurre Bosc pears (480g), thinly sliced lengthways

1 cup (100g) walnuts, roasted

150g soft goat's cheese, crumbled

1/4 cup (10g) small mint leaves

1/2 tsp dried chilli flakes

salt and freshly ground black pepper

pickled fennel

1 large fennel bulb (550g)

1 tbsp sea salt flakes

1/3 cup (80ml) white wine vinegar

2 tsp caster sugar

1 Put the lentils and 3 cups (750ml) cold tap water in a medium saucepan; bring to the boil. Reduce the heat to low; cook, partially covered by a lid, for 12 minutes or until the lentils are tender and the water has been absorbed. Remove from the heat. Add 1 tablespoon of the olive oil; season with salt and pepper to taste. Stir in the parsley; set aside.

2 To make the pickled fennel, trim the ends from the fennel, reserving 2 tablespoons of the fronds. Cut the fennel bulb in half lengthways. Using a mandolin, V-slicer, or sharp knife, cut the fennel into very thin slices. Put in a colander with 2 teaspoons of the sea salt; allow to stand for 10 minutes. Rinse off the salt, then squeeze out any excess water. Transfer the fennel to a large bowl. Combine the remaining salt, vinegar, and sugar in a jug, stirring to dissolve the salt and sugar. Pour over the fennel; toss gently. Cover and refrigerate until needed.

3 Preheat a frying pan to a high heat. Toss the pear slices with 1 tablespoon of the olive oil in a large bowl; season with a good grinding of pepper. Cook the pear slices for 3 minutes on each side or until browned.

4 Drain the pickled fennel; reserve the pickling liquid. To serve, layer the pear slices, lentils, and pickled fennel on a platter. Scatter with the walnuts, goat's cheese, mint, chilli flakes, and reserved fennel fronds. Drizzle with the reserved pickling liquid and remaining olive oil. Season with salt and pepper to taste.

TIPS

▪ Try Golden Delicious or Pink Lady apples instead of the pear and pecans halves instead of walnuts.

▪ To keep the recipe healthy, stick with fresh cheeses such as bocconcini (mozzarella balls) or labneh if using in place of the goat's cheese.

Curry-roasted aubergine with dhal salad

VEGETARIAN/HIGH-FIBRE | PREP + COOK TIME **35 MINUTES** | SERVES **4**

PER SERVING | Energy kcals 314 | Carbohydrate 17g of which sugar 7g | Fat 20g of which saturates 6g | Salt 0.49g plus seasoning | Fibre 9g

Packed with dietary fibre, aubergines are a good source of B vitamins, as well as potassium, magnesium, and other minerals. Lentils up not only the fibre content of this dish, but also its essential nutrients quotient. If you cannot find finger aubergines, cut a large aubergine into thick wedges instead. You can also make the recipe with other curry pastes such as korma.

6 finger aubergines (720g), halved lengthways

2 tbsp tandoori paste

2 tbsp extra virgin olive oil

$^1/_2$ cucumber (65g)

$^3/_4$ cup (210g) Greek-style yogurt

1 garlic clove, crushed

400g can brown lentils, drained, rinsed

2 cups (80g) pea shoots

2 tbsp lemon juice

salt and freshly ground black pepper

$^1/_3$ cup (50g) roasted unsalted cashews, chopped, to serve

1   Preheat the oven to 200°C (180°C fan/400°F/Gas 6). Line a large baking tray with baking parchment.

2   Using a sharp knife, score the cut sides of the aubergines in a crisscross pattern. Place the aubergines, cut-side up, on the prepared tray. Combine the tandoori paste and olive oil; season with salt and pepper to taste. Spread over the cut side of the aubergines.

3   Roast the aubergines, cut-side up, for 15 minutes. Turn and cook for a further 10 minutes or until tender.

4   Meanwhile, coarsely grate the cucumber; squeeze out any excess liquid. Combine the cucumber, yogurt, and garlic in a small bowl. Season with salt and pepper to taste.

5   Put the lentils, pea shoots, and lemon juice in a medium bowl; toss through. Season with salt and pepper to taste. Arrange the aubergines on a platter; spoon over the dhal salad and cucumber-yogurt. Serve with the roasted cashews sprinkled over the top.

WHOLESOME
DINNERS

Here, you'll find plenty of filling and
nutritious energy-boosting recipes to feed
family and friends, from weeknight staples to
healthier twists on comfort-food classics.

Baked carrot, haloumi, and mint patties

FAST | PREP + COOK TIME **35 MINUTES** | MAKES **12**

PER SERVING | Energy kcals 170 | Carbohydrate 12g of which sugar 6g | Fat 9g of which saturates 3g | Salt 0.8g plus seasoning | Fibre 4g

Beta carotene is what makes carrots, sweet potato, and pumpkin orange. Beta carotene can also be converted to vitamin A in the body. While diets rich in beta carotene have been shown to benefit health, supplements do not have the same effect and can be harmful. Stick to real foods to gain all the benefits without any of the risks.

6 large carrots (1kg), coarsely grated

6 spring onions, thinly sliced

180g haloumi, coarsely grated

3 cups (150g) coarsely chopped mint leaves, plus extra sprigs, to serve

²/₃ cup (100g) wholemeal plain flour

4 eggs, lightly beaten

extra virgin olive oil cooking spray

4 cups (120g) trimmed watercress sprigs

¹/₂ cup (120g) ready-made baba ghanoush

salt and freshly ground black pepper

extra virgin olive oil for drizzling (optional)

1 Preheat the oven to 220°C (200°C fan/425°F/Gas 7). Line 2 baking trays with baking parchment.

2 Put the carrots, spring onions, haloumi, 3 cups (150g) mint leaves, flour, and eggs in a large bowl; stir to combine. Season with salt and pepper to taste.

3 Using a ¹/₂-cup (125ml) measure, divide the mixture into 12 portions. Place the portions 4cm apart on the prepared trays; shape and flatten into 8cm patties. Spray generously with the extra virgin olive oil.

4 Bake the patties for 30 minutes, swapping and rotating trays between shelves once during the cooking time.

5 Serve the baked patties with the watercress and extra mint sprigs; accompany with the baba ghanoush, drizzled with extra virgin olive oil, if you like.

TIP

Serve the patties stuffed into wholemeal pitta bread pockets or wrapped in Mountain Bread or other handkerchief-style flatbread, if you like.

Kidney bean, prawn, and pepper fajita wraps

FAST | PREP + COOK TIME **20 MINUTES** | SERVES **4**

PER SERVING | Energy kcals 444 | Carbohydrate 39g of which sugar 12g | Fat 13g of which saturates 4g | Salt 1.3g plus seasoning | Fibre 11g

Prawns provide good levels of the long-chain omega-3 fats you might be taking as a fish oil supplement. These fats are crucially important when it comes to the brain and seem to play a role in cognitive function and brain health as we age.

600g (1¼ lb) medium uncooked prawns, peeled, deveined, tails intact

2 tbsp extra virgin olive oil

1 tbsp Tabasco chipotle sauce, plus extra ½ tsp

1 tsp smoked paprika

1 red onion (170g), sliced into thin wedges

1 red pepper, deseeded, sliced

1 yellow pepper, deseeded, sliced

400g can pinto beans, drained, rinsed

400g mixed cherry tomatoes, halved

4 medium wholegrain tortillas (160g)

½ cup (120g) light soured cream

salt and freshly ground black pepper

½ cup (15g) coriander leaves, to serve

1 Preheat a ridged cast-iron grill plate or barbecue to a high heat.

2 Thread the prawns onto 8 metal or soaked bamboo skewers; place on a tray. Put the olive oil, 1 tablespoon Tabasco chipotle sauce, and paprika in a small bowl; mix well. Season with salt and pepper to taste. Brush 1½ tablespoons of the marinade over the prawn skewers.

3 Heat the remaining marinade in a large frying pan over a high heat. Add the onion and sliced peppers; cook, stirring occasionally, for 4 minutes or until starting to turn golden and soften.

4 Add the pinto beans, tomatoes, and ¼ cup (60ml) water to the pan; stir well. Cook for 4 minutes or until hot and saucelike.

5 Meanwhile, barbecue the prawn skewers for 1 minute on each side or until cooked through and grill marks appear. Barbecue the tortillas for 30 seconds on each side or until grill marks appear.

6 Divide the red and yellow pepper mixture among the tortillas; top each one with the barbecued prawns, soured cream, and a drizzle of the extra ½ teaspoon Tabasco chipotle sauce. Serve the fajitas hot, with the coriander leaves scattered over the filling.

Yogurt, kabocha squash, and pistachio pie

VEGETARIAN | PREP + COOK TIME **1 HOUR 20 MINUTES** | SERVES **4**

PER SERVING | Energy kcals 510 | Carbohydrate 41g of which sugar 8g | Fat 28g of which saturates 9g | Salt 0.8g plus seasoning | Fibre 6g

Lutein and zeaxanthin are found in high concentrations in the eye and seem to play a crucial role in eye health. Those people with diets high in these two carotenoids reduce their risk of macular degeneration and developing cataracts. You'll find them in dark, leafy greens and cos lettuce, as well as in egg yolks.

500g kabocha squash (Japanese pumpkin), peeled, cut into 2cm pieces

1 tbsp extra virgin olive oil

$^1/_3$ cup (45g) pistachios

2 tbsp tahini

1$^1/_4$ cups (350g) Greek-style yogurt

2 eggs

2 tbsp fresh dill sprigs

extra virgin olive oil cooking spray

6 sheets of fresh filo pastry (see tip)

$^1/_4$ tsp sumac

240g mixed salad leaves

salt and freshly ground black pepper

1 Preheat the oven to 180°C (160°C fan/350°F/Gas 4). Position an oven shelf to sit on the lowest rung of the oven.

2 Put the kabocha squash and olive oil in a medium microwave-safe bowl; stir through to coat the squash with the oil. Season with salt and pepper to taste. Cover with cling film; microwave on HIGH (100%), stirring halfway through, for 4 minutes 15 seconds or until just softened. Drain to remove any liquid; set aside to cool slightly.

3 Process the pistachios and tahini until smooth. Add the yogurt, eggs, and 1 tablespoon of the dill; pulse until well combined. Transfer the yogurt mixture to a large jug; stir through the cooled squash. Season with salt and pepper to taste.

4 Lightly spray a 22cm springform tin with the extra virgin olive oil cooking spray. Place a sheet of filo over the top of the tin, then place a second sheet on top in the opposite direction; spray again with the olive oil. Repeat layering and spraying the remaining sheets of filo pastry. Gently press the layered pastry into the tin, leaving the pastry edges overhanging the top edge.

5 Pour the squash filling into the pastry case, and gently shake the tin to evenly distribute the pieces of squash. Fold in the excess pastry, scrunching it slightly to cover the filling. Spray with extra virgin olive oil.

6 Bake the pie on the lowest shelf in the oven for 1 hour or until the filling is just set and the pastry is golden. Remove from the tin immediately to prevent the pastry from steaming and becoming soggy. Top the pie with the remaining dill; dust with the sumac. Serve with the lettuce leaves.

TIPS

• You can swap sweet potatoes for the squash and almonds for the pistachios, if you like.

• Fresh filo pastry, found in the refrigerated section of the supermarket, is less brittle than frozen filo, and therefore less likely to tear as you work with it. If you cannot find chilled fresh filo pastry, use thawed frozen filo instead.

Salmon and olive salsa verde with fennel and Swiss chard salad

HEALTHY FATS | PREP **25 MINUTES** | SERVES **4**

PER SERVING | Energy kcals 822 | Carbohydrate 26g of which sugar 9g | Fat 57g of which saturates 9g | Salt 1.9g plus seasoning | Fibre 13g

People who are members of cultures where a lot of fish and seafood is traditionally eaten have lower levels of depression. There is ongoing research into this area, but there is certainly some evidence to suggest that upping the intake of omega-3s such as those found in salmon can help to reduce depressive symptoms in some people.

2½ tbsp extra virgin olive oil

1 orange sweet potato (400g), skin on, thinly sliced lengthways

4 x 200g boneless salmon fillets, skin on

1 large fennel bulb (550g), thinly sliced

4 Swiss chard leaves (240g), finely shredded

sea salt and freshly ground black pepper

green olive salsa verde

³/₄ cup (135g) pitted Sicilian green olives

1 tbsp baby capers

1 garlic clove

3 cups (60g) flat-leaf parsley leaves

1 tbsp red wine vinegar

¹/₃ cup (80ml) extra virgin olive oil

1   Heat 2 tablespoons of the olive oil in a large non-stick frying pan over a high heat. Cook the sweet potato, in batches, for 1 minute on each side or until golden and cooked through. Transfer to a baking tray lined with kitchen paper; season with salt and pepper to taste.

2   Heat the remaining olive oil in the same pan over a high heat. Sprinkle the salmon skin with sea salt and a good grinding of pepper. Cook the salmon, skin-side down, for 4 minutes or until the skin is crisp. Turn; cook for a further 2 minutes or until the salmon is just cooked through.

3   Meanwhile, to make the green olive salsa verde, process the olives, capers, garlic, and parsley until finely chopped. Add the vinegar, olive oil, and ¹/₃ cup (80ml) water; process until well combined.

4   Put the fennel, Swiss chard, and ½ cup (125ml) of the green olive salsa verde in a large bowl; toss to mix through.

5   Divide the salmon, sweet potato, and fennel salad among 4 serving plates. Serve with the remaining salsa verde.

Ricotta, asparagus, broad bean, and mint risotto

HIGH-FIBRE | PREP + COOK TIME **55 MINUTES** | SERVES **4**

PER SERVING | Energy kcals 536 | Carbohydrate 65g of which sugar 6g | Fat 20g of which saturates 6g | Salt 0.2g | Fibre 10g

Brown rice retains the bran and germ, which are removed during the milling process for white rice. Both types of rice are high in carbohydrates; however, the wholegrain nature of brown rice adds extra fibre, plus more vitamins and minerals, than its white counterpart.

340g fresh asparagus, trimmed

1 litre (4 cups) vegetable stock

$^1/_4$ cup (60ml) extra virgin olive oil

1 white onion (150g), finely chopped

2 garlic cloves, crushed

1$^1/_2$ cups (300g) brown rice

1 cup (25g) firmly packed mint leaves

$^3/_4$ cup (180g) soft fresh ricotta

1$^1/_2$ cups (225g) frozen broad beans, thawed, peeled

1 large lemon (200g)

$^1/_3$ cup (25g) finely grated Parmesan

freshly ground black pepper

1 Cut the asparagus spears into 10cm lengths; halve or quarter lengthwise depending on the thickness. Thinly slice the remaining bottom half of the asparagus into rounds.

2 Pour the vegetable stock and 1$^1/_2$ cups (375ml) water into a medium saucepan; bring to the boil over a high heat. Reduce the heat to low; keep at a gentle simmer.

3 Meanwhile, heat 2 tablespoons of the olive oil in a large, heavy-based saucepan over a medium heat. Cook the onion and garlic, stirring frequently, for 2 minutes or until softened. Add the rice; stir to coat the grains in the mixture.

4 Add three-quarters of the hot stock mixture to the pan; remove the remaining stock (still in the pan) from the heat. Cook the risotto, covered, over a low heat, for 35 minutes, or until the liquid has been absorbed and the rice is tender. Stir the rice a few times during the cooking time to ensure it is not sticking to the bottom of the pan.

5 Meanwhile, add the asparagus spears to the remaining stock; bring back to the boil. Simmer for 1 minute until just tender. Remove from the heat. Using a pair of tongs, transfer the asparagus to a plate. Reserve stock.

6 Reserve 2 tablespoons of the small mint leaves to serve. Process the remaining mint and the ricotta until smooth.

7 Uncover the rice; increase the heat to high. Stir through the remaining stock, asparagus rounds and broad beans. Cook, stirring frequently, for 10 minutes or until thickened.

8 Grate 2 teaspoons zest from the lemon; squeeze the juice from the lemon (you will need 2 teaspoons). Add the ricotta mixture, Parmesan, lemon zest, and juice to the risotto; stir to combine. Season with pepper. Top with the asparagus spears, reserved mint leaves, and remaining olive oil.

TIPS

- Customize the vegetables to your taste and to the season. Try broccolini (Tenderstem broccoli) instead of asparagus and peas instead of broad beans.
- To make this dish vegetarian, use a suitable vegetarian hard cheese in place of the Parmesan.

One-pan pork and almond meatballs with kale and broccolini

HIGH-PROTEIN | PREP **25 MINUTES** | SERVES **4**

PER SERVING | Energy kcals 477 | Carbohydrate 8g of which sugar 7g | Fat 31g of which saturates 7g | Salt 0.7g plus seasoning | Fibre 4g

Kale is one of the most nutritious leafy greens. It's particularly rich in carotenoids that can be converted to vitamin A in the body. A single cup of kale provides you with more than 200 per cent of your daily recommended amount of vitamin A.

$1/2$ cup (80g) blanched almonds, roasted, plus extra, to serve

500g pork mince

2 garlic cloves, crushed

1 egg

$1/4$ cup (7g) finely chopped tarragon, plus extra 3 sprigs

2 tsp finely grated lemon zest

$1/3$ cup (25g) finely grated Parmesan, plus extra, to serve

2 tsp extra virgin olive oil

$2^1/2$ cups (625ml) almond milk

1 tbsp Dijon mustard

175g broccolini (Tenderstem broccoli), blanched, trimmed, halved lengthways

1 bunch of kale (250g), trimmed, chopped

salt and freshly ground black pepper

1 Put the $1/2$ cup (80g) almonds in a small food processor; process until finely chopped. Combine the pork, almonds, garlic, egg, $1/4$ cup (6g) tarragon, lemon zest, and $1/3$ cup (25g) Parmesan in a large bowl; season with salt and pepper to taste. Roll into tablespoon-sized balls.

2 Heat the olive oil in a large, deep-sided frying pan over a medium heat. Add the meatballs and cook, turning, for 4 minutes or until browned.

3 Add the almond milk, extra 3 sprigs of tarragon, and Dijon mustard; bring to a simmer. Cook for 6 minutes or until the sauce has reduced slightly; season with salt and pepper to taste.

4 Add the broccolini and kale; gently toss. Cook for 2 minutes; season with salt and pepper to taste. Serve with the extra almonds and Parmesan sprinkled over the top.

TIP

To blanch the broccolini (Tenderstem broccoli), place in a heatproof bowl; cover with boiling water. Allow to stand for 2 minutes; drain.

Donburi with mushrooms and salmon

HIGH-PROTEIN | PREP + COOK TIME **35 MINUTES** | MAKES **12**

PER SERVING | Energy kcals 577 | Carbohydrate 39g of which sugar 6g | Fat 30g of which saturates 5g | Salt 2.8g | Fibre 4.5g

The Japanese dish donburi is named after its cooking style and the type of bowl in which it is served. Ingredients vary, from fish and meat to vegetables, but they are always simmered in a sauce and served over rice. Here, it is the rice that absorbs the sauce. Mushrooms provide B vitamins and essential minerals; ginger and garlic both contain powerful antioxidants.

500g microwave or instant brown rice and quinoa

2 tbsp extra virgin olive oil

300g mixed Asian mushrooms such as oyster, shiitake, and enoki, large mushrooms halved

4 spring onions, thinly sliced

1 tbsp grated fresh root ginger

2 garlic cloves, crushed

1 long red chilli, seeded, finely chopped

1/4 cup (60ml) light soy sauce

2 tbsp sake

1 tbsp mirin

4 x 130g boneless salmon fillets, skin on

to serve

sliced long red chilli

sliced spring onion

lime wedges

1 Heat the rice and quinoa mix according to the packet directions.

2 Next, heat half of the olive oil in a wok over a high heat; stir-fry the mushrooms for 3 minutes or until lightly golden. Add the spring onions, ginger, garlic, and finely chopped chilli; stir-fry for a further 1 minute until fragrant. Add the combined soy sauce, sake and mirin with the rice-quinoa mixture; stir-fry until combined.

3 Meanwhile, heat the remaining olive oil in a large frying pan over a high heat; cook the salmon fillets, skin-side down, for 3 minutes or until the skin is crisp. Turn and cook for a further 2 minutes for medium rare or until the salmon is cooked to your liking.

4 Divide the rice mixture among 4 serving bowls; top with the salmon. Serve topped with the extra sliced chilli and spring onion, with lime wedges for squeezing over.

Aubergine and courgette yogurt bake

VEGETARIAN | PREP + COOK TIME **1 HOUR 15 MINUTES** | SERVES **4**

PER SERVING | Energy kcals 658 | Carbohydrate 31g of which sugar 21g | Fat 45g of which saturates 21g | Salt 1.3g plus seasoning | Fibre 8g

Tomatoes contain the carotenoid lycopene, an antioxidant that gives them their red colour, and may be useful in reducing the risk of some cancers and heart disease. While cooking does slightly reduce the vitamin C content in tomatoes, it actually increases the lycopene content.

2 aubergines (600g), cut into 2.5cm pieces

1 onion (150g), thinly sliced

1/4 cup (60ml) extra virgin olive oil

1 tbsp cumin seeds

2 x 130g packets cherry vine tomatoes

2 courgettes (240g), cut into 2cm pieces

400g can cherry tomatoes

1/4 cup (7g) oregano leaves, finely chopped

1/4 cup (45g) rice flour

3 cups (840g) Greek-style yogurt

3 eggs

120g marinated feta, drained

salt and freshly ground black pepper

1 Preheat the oven to 220°C (200°C fan/425°F/Gas 7). Place a large baking tray in the oven; heat for 5 minutes.

2 Put the aubergines, onion, 1 tablespoon of the olive oil, and cumin seeds on the hot tray; season well with salt and a good grinding of pepper. Arrange the vine tomatoes on top; roast the vegetables for 10 minutes.

3 Remove the vine tomatoes, and set aside to serve. Add the courgettes, canned tomatoes, and half of the oregano to the tray with the vegetables; stir to mix through. Roast for a further 15 minutes or until golden.

4 Spoon the aubergine mixture into four 16cm (1 1/2-cup/375ml) round ovenproof dishes. Set aside.

5 Heat the remaining olive oil in a medium saucepan over a medium heat. Add the rice flour and whisk for 2 minutes, or until the mixture is pale and frothy. Remove the pan from the heat; whisk in the yogurt and eggs until combined.

6 Spoon the yogurt mixture over the vegetables in the dishes, dividing it among them evenly; sprinkle over the feta. Bake for 18 minutes or until golden and bubbling. Serve topped with the roasted vine tomatoes and the remaining oregano leaves.

TIP

If you would like to reduce the fat content of this dish, switch to a high-protein no-fat thick Greek-style yogurt in place of the full-fat yogurt above. Alternatively, use a 50:50 mix of fresh ricotta and yogurt, or even 2 parts ricotta to 1 part yogurt.

Korean-style prawn pancakes

HIGH-PROTEIN | PREP + COOK TIME **40 MINUTES** | SERVES **4**

PER SERVING | Energy kcals 825 | Carbohydrate 73g of which sugar 8g | Fat 28g of which saturates 5g | Salt 2.3g plus seasoning | Fibre 10g

Spring onion pancakes, or *pajeon*, are a Korean favourite. Usually made with a mixture of wheat and rice flours, they are large fritter-like pancakes chockful of fresh ingredients. For a vegetarian version of the pancakes, use a flavoured tofu or tempeh, cut into cubes or batons.

2 cups (320g) wholemeal plain flour

1/3 cup (60g) brown rice flour

4 eggs

2 tbsp sesame seeds, toasted

1/3 cup (80ml) kecap manis (sweet soy sauce)

2 tbsp lime juice

1/4 cup (60ml) extra virgin olive oil

1kg uncooked prawns, shelled, deveined, halved horizontally

8 spring onions, trimmed, quartered lengthways

1/3 cup (15g) finely chopped coriander leaves and stems, plus extra leaves, to serve (optional)

salt and freshly ground black pepper

1 In a large bowl, whisk together the flours, 2 1/2 cups (625ml) ice-cold water, eggs, and 1 tablespoon of the sesame seeds until just combined; season with salt and pepper to taste. Refrigerate the batter for 10 minutes.

2 Meanwhile, put the kecap manis and lime juice in a screw-top jar with a tight-fitting lid; shake well to combine. Set aside until needed.

3 Heat 1 tablespoon of the olive oil in a 23cm (base measurement) ovenproof non-stick frying pan over a high heat; cook the prawns, in batches, for 1 minute or until just cooked through and lightly golden. Transfer to a bowl.

4 Preheat the grill to a high heat.

5 Heat 2 teaspoons of the olive oil in the same pan over a medium heat; pour in one-quarter of the batter; top with one-quarter each of the spring onions, cooked prawns, and coriander. Cook, covered, for 3 minutes or until the bottom is set.

6 Transfer the pancake (still in the pan) to the oven; grill for a further 1 minute or until lightly golden and cooked through. Slide the pancake onto a plate; cover to keep warm. Repeat with the remaining ingredients to make 4 pancakes in total.

7 Drizzle the pancakes with the kecap manis dressing; scatter with the remaining sesame seeds. Serve topped with extra coriander leaves, if you like.

TIPS

- Serve the pancakes topped with curled spring onion tops and micro herbs, if you like.
- Kecap manis is an Indonesian soy sauce sweetened with palm sugar, which gives it a distinctive flavour and a thick, syrupy consistency.

Broccolini pasta with gooey eggs

VEGETARIAN | PREP + COOK TIME **30 MINUTES** | SERVES **4**

PER SERVING | Energy kcals 571 | Carbohydrate 50g of which sugar 4g | Fat 26g of which saturates 5g | Salt 0.4g plus seasoning | Fibre 10g

Brief cooking is the best way to preserve the nutrients in green vegetables such as broccolini and other brassicas. You can also throw them into dishes in the last moments of cooking until just softened. If you cook them for too long, not only won't they taste very nice, but they'll lose their bright green colour as well.

300g dried buckwheat pasta

6 eggs, at room temperature

2 tbsp extra virgin olive oil

$\frac{1}{2}$ cup (60g) finely chopped walnuts

2 garlic cloves, thinly sliced

1 long red chilli, seeded, finely chopped

350g broccolini (Tenderstem broccoli), trimmed, halved lengthways

1 large lemon (200g)

salt and freshly ground black pepper

1 Fill a large bowl with ice cubes and water. Place near the hob.

2 Bring a large saucepan of salted water to the boil. Add the buckwheat pasta, return to the boil, and cook for 2 minutes. Carefully add the eggs and cook with the pasta, keeping on the boil, for a further 6 minutes. Using a slotted spoon, transfer the eggs to the iced water.

3 Meanwhile, heat the olive oil in a large frying pan over a low-medium heat; cook the walnuts, garlic, and chilli, stirring, for 3 minutes or until the garlic and walnuts are lightly golden. Season with salt and pepper to taste.

4 Add the broccolini to the saucepan with the pasta; cook for 1 minute or until the pasta and broccolini are both just tender.

5 Drain the pasta and broccolini; reserve $\frac{1}{2}$ cup (125ml) of the cooking water. Grate 2 teaspoons zest from the lemon, then squeeze the juice from it (you will need $\frac{1}{4}$ cup/60ml of lemon juice). Add the pasta and broccolini to the walnut mixture with the lemon zest and juice. Season with salt and pepper to taste; toss well.

6 Divide the pasta among 4 serving bowls. Peel the eggs; break open over each bowl of pasta, allowing the soft yolks to disperse as a sauce.

Beans and tofu with pitta crisps

HIGH-PROTEIN | PREP + COOK TIME **35 MINUTES** | SERVES **4**

PER SERVING | Energy kcals 910 | Carbohydrate 113g of which sugar 28g | Fat 27g of which saturates 4g | Salt 2.9g plus seasoning | Fibre 24g

Chickpeas are a great source of protein, complex carbohydrates, minerals, and several vitamins. Serving the chickpeas with wholegrain pitta breads as in this recipe also means you will get the full spectrum of essential amino acids.

$1/3$ cup (80ml) extra virgin olive oil

300g firm tofu, coarsely crumbled

$1/2$ tsp chilli flakes

1 cup (25g) firmly packed flat-leaf parsley, half coarsely chopped

1 large red onion (300g), thinly sliced

2 carrots (240g), coarsely grated

2 x 400g cans cherry tomatoes

400g can chickpeas, drained, rinsed

400g can black beans, drained, rinsed

2 tbsp Worcestershire sauce

2 tbsp Dijon mustard

2 tbsp pure maple syrup

4 oval wholemeal pitta bread pockets

salt and freshly ground black pepper

1 Heat 2 tablespoons of the olive oil in a large frying pan over a medium heat; cook the tofu, turning frequently, for 6 minutes or until golden. Add the chilli and chopped parsley; cook for 30 seconds. Transfer with a slotted spoon to a plate lined with kitchen paper. Set aside to keep warm.

2 Return the pan to the heat. Add 1 tablespoon of the olive oil; cook the onion for 5 minutes or until starting to brown.

3 Add the carrots, tomatoes, chickpeas, black beans, Worcestershire sauce, Dijon mustard, and maple syrup to the pan; cook, stirring occasionally, for 20 minutes or until the mixture is thickened. Season with salt and pepper to taste.

4 Meanwhile, preheat the grill to a high heat. Place a large wire rack over a large baking tray. Cut the pitta breads in half horizontally; brush with the remaining olive oil. Grill in 2 batches, cut-side up, for 4 minutes or until golden. Remove and keep warm.

5 Serve the pitta crisps topped with the bean mixture, crisp tofu, and remaining parsley leaves.

TIPS

- You can swap the black beans for kidney beans instead, if you like.
- To make this dish vegetarian, choose a vegetarian version of Worcestershire sauce such as Henderson's Relish.

Veggie patch pies

HIGH-FIBRE | PREP + COOK TIME **1 HOUR 15 MINUTES** | SERVES **4**

PER SERVING | Energy kcals 776 | Carbohydrate 84g of which sugar 21g | Fat 33g of which saturates 5g | Salt 1.8g plus seasoning | Fibre 18g

This recipe has it all: a good array of vegetables and protein, and fibre from the beans and oats. As a bonus, the walnuts offer a veritable array of antioxidant and anti-inflammatory nutrients, as well as valuable monounsaturated and hard-to-source omega-3 fatty acids.

1 large orange sweet potato (500g)

5 large flat mushrooms (400g)

1 aubergine (300g)

2 tbsp extra virgin olive oil

1 tsp ground cumin

1 tsp paprika

400g can black beans, drained, rinsed

400g can red kidney beans, drained, rinsed

2 cups (560g) tomato pasta sauce

salt and freshly ground black pepper

pie topping

1 wholemeal pitta bread pocket (150g)

1/2 cup (45g) rolled oats

1/2 cup (50g) walnuts

1/4 cup (60ml) extra virgin olive oil

1/3 cup (25g) finely grated Parmesan

1 1/2 tbsp thyme leaves

1 Preheat the oven to 220°C (200°C fan/425°F/Gas 7). Line 2 large baking trays with baking parchment.

2 Cut the sweet potato into 2.5cm pieces. Cut the mushrooms and aubergine into 2cm pieces. Toss the vegetables with the oil and spices in a bowl; season well with salt and a good grinding of pepper. Arrange in a single layer over the prepared trays. Roast for 30 minutes or until the vegetables are soft and golden brown, swapping the trays between shelves halfway through the cooking time.

3 Meanwhile, to make the pie topping, coarsely tear the pitta bread; process with half of the rolled oats, half of the walnuts, and the olive oil until coarsely chopped and combined. Stir through the Parmesan, 1 tablespoon of the thyme leaves, and the remaining rolled oats and walnuts.

4 Combine the black beans, red kidney beans, pasta sauce, and 2 tablespoons water in a large bowl. Stir through the hot cooked vegetables; season with salt and pepper to taste. Divide the mixture evenly among four 2-cup (500ml) ovenproof dishes. Next, divide the topping among the dishes.

5 Bake the pies for 20 minutes or until the tops are golden and the filling is bubbling. Serve topped with the remaining thyme leaves.

Cauliflower 'butter chicken'

VEGETARIAN | PREP + COOK TIME **40 MINUTES** | SERVES **4**

PER SERVING | Energy kcals 436 | Carbohydrate 30g of which sugar 19g | Fat 26g of which saturates 6g | Salt 0.2g plus seasoning | Fibre 10g

Cauliflower replaces chicken in this vegetarian take on butter chicken. Numerous studies have shown that members of the *Brassica* genus, which includes cauliflower, offer some protection against cancers, heart disease, and the functional declines associated with ageing.

1 cauliflower (1.5kg)

$1/4$ cup (60ml) extra virgin olive oil

1 onion (150g), finely chopped

2 garlic cloves, crushed

1 tbsp grated fresh root ginger

$1/4$ cup (10g) finely chopped coriander leaves and stems, plus extra leaves, to serve

1 tsp garam masala

1 tsp ground cumin

1 tsp smoked paprika

1 cinnamon stick

400g passata

1 cup (250ml) vegetable stock

$1/2$ cup (140g) Greek-style yogurt

$1/2$ cup (75g) unsalted roasted cashews

salt and freshly ground black pepper

steamed rice, to serve

1 Cut the cauliflower into medium-sized florets. Heat 2 tablespoons of the olive oil in a large, deep frying pan over a medium heat; cook the cauliflower, in 2 batches and turning occasionally, for 10 minutes or until dark golden and cooked through. Remove the cauliflower from the pan; wipe the pan clean.

2 Heat the remaining olive oil in the same pan over a medium heat; cook the onion for 5 minutes or until softened. Add the garlic, ginger, chopped coriander, and spices; cook for 30 seconds or until fragrant.

3 Add the passata and vegetable stock; bring to a simmer and cook, covered, for 10 minutes. Stir through the yogurt. Season with salt and pepper to taste. Add the cauliflower to the sauce; cook for 5 minutes or until warmed through.

4 Scatter the cauliflower 'butter chicken' with the cashews and extra coriander leaves. Serve with steamed rice.

Golden cauliflower gnocchi with Swiss chard

VEGETARIAN/LOW-CARB | PREP + COOK TIME **50 MINUTES** | SERVES **4**

PER SERVING | Energy kcals 311 | Carbohydrate 22g of which sugar 12g | Fat 8g of which saturates 1.5g | Salt 2.2g plus seasoning | Fibre 9g

Cauliflower is a versatile vegetable, making it a great low-carb alternative for typically high-carb ingredients such as rice and dishes such as gnocchi. In the recipe here, it replaces potatoes and white flour for a delicious gnocchi with Swiss chard and hazelnuts.

1kg cauliflower, cut into 3cm florets (see tip)

1^1/$_2$ cups (225g) white spelt flour, plus extra, to dust

^{1}/$_4$ tsp ground nutmeg

^{1}/$_3$ cup (80ml) extra virgin olive oil, plus extra for greasing

1 bunch of Swiss chard (750g), stems very thinly sliced, leaves torn

2 tsp finely grated lemon zest

2 tbsp lemon juice

^{1}/$_3$ cup (45g) coarsely chopped toasted hazelnuts

^{1}/$_2$ tsp dried chilli flakes

salt and freshly ground black pepper

1 Steam the cauliflower in a covered steamer basket, over a saucepan of boiling water, for 8 minutes or until tender. Transfer the cauliflower to a clean tea towel; allow to cool for 5 minutes. Squeeze out as much excess liquid as possible, until the cauliflower feels dry.

2 Process the cauliflower with the spelt flour, nutmeg, and salt and pepper to taste until the mixture just comes together as a ball of dough. Turn out the dough onto a lightly floured work surface; knead gently until smooth. Cut the dough into 4 equal portions. Cover with a clean tea towel.

3 Roll each dough portion into a 2cm thick rope, about 29cm long. Cut into 2cm pieces. Transfer to a lightly floured tray.

4 Cook the gnocchi, in batches, in a large saucepan of boiling salted water for 3 minutes or until the gnocchi float to the surface. Remove the gnocchi from the pan with a slotted spoon. Transfer to an oiled tray. Reserve ^{1}/$_2$ cup (125ml) of the cooking water.

5 Heat 2 tablespoons of the olive oil in a large, deep frying pan over a medium heat. Cook the gnocchi, tossing, for 3 minutes or until golden brown. Remove from the pan; set aside to keep warm. Heat the remaining oil in the same pan over a medium heat. Cook the chard stems for 3 minutes or until almost soft. Add the chard leaves and reserved cooking water. Cook, stirring, for 1 minute until just wilted. Stir in the lemon zest and juice. Season well with salt and a good grinding of pepper, and remove the pan from the heat.

6 Divide the chard mixture among 4 serving bowls. Top with the gnocchi, and sprinkle over the chopped hazelnuts and chilli flakes to serve.

TIP

Once you have trimmed the cauliflower, weigh it, as you will need 850g to make the gnocchi.

Sides

Each of these side dishes is more than an afterthought for expanding a meal to something more substantial – and more than just a quick way to get more vegetables onto a plate. Filled with vibrant, health-boosting ingredients, they will tempt even the fussiest eater.

Sweet potato and chickpea mash

PREP + COOK TIME **30 MINUTES** | SERVES **4**

Peel and coarsely chop 1kg orange sweet potatoes. Put the sweet potato in a medium saucepan with enough cold water to just cover. Boil over a medium heat for 15 minutes or until the sweet potato is tender; drain. Add a drained and rinsed 400g can chickpeas during the last 5 minutes of the cooking time to heat through. Return the sweet potato mixture to the pan; mash until smooth (or use a potato ricer or mouli). Add 2 tablespoons garlic-infused olive oil, 1 tablespoon tahini, and 1 tablespoon lemon juice; fold in gently until the mash is smooth. Season with salt and freshly ground black pepper to taste.

Broccoli and cauliflower rice

PREP + COOK TIME **15 MINUTES** | SERVES **4**

Trim the ends of 750g broccoli stalks; discard. Cut the broccoli into florets. Remove the outside leaves, base, and any tough, thick stalks from 750g cauliflower; discard. Cut the cauliflower into florets. Using a food processor, pulse the florets, in small batches, with $\frac{1}{4}$ teaspoon sea salt flakes until the consistency of rice. Working in batches, place the vegetable 'rice' in the centre of a clean tea towel. Gather the ends of the cloth together to enclose the rice, then twist, squeezing tightly, to remove as much excess moisture as possible. The broccoli and cauliflower rice can be eaten raw in salads or stir-fried like rice.

Garlicky green beans and peas with pine nuts

PREP + COOK TIME **15 MINUTES** | SERVES **4**

Trim 200g each of baby green beans, sugarsnap peas, and mangetout. Bring a large saucepan of salted water to the boil. Place a small sieve over a small stainless-steel bowl. Stir 2 thinly sliced large garlic cloves, 2 tablespoons pine nuts, and $\frac{1}{4}$ cup (60ml) extra virgin olive oil in a non-stick frying pan over a medium heat for 4 minutes until the garlic is golden. Strain into a bowl; reserve the oil. Whisk 2 teaspoons Dijon mustard and 1 tablespoon lemon juice into the reserved oil. Cook the beans for 1 minute. Add the sugarsnap peas; cook for a further 1 minute. Add the mangetout; cook for a further minute. Drain; refresh under cold water. Toss the greens with the dressing. Serve scattered with the reserved garlic and pine nuts. Season with salt and freshly ground black pepper.

Corn in the husk with Parmesan

PREP + COOK TIME **15 MINUTES** | SERVES **4**

Cook 6 sweetcorn cobs (1.5kg) in husks in a large saucepan of boiling salted water for 8 minutes until almost tender. Drain; cool in the husks. Peel back the husks; discard silks. Tie back the husks with kitchen string. Meanwhile, heat $\frac{1}{4}$ cup (60ml) extra virgin olive oil in a small pan. Add 1 crushed garlic clove, 2 tablespoons chopped pine nuts, 1 teaspoon salt, and $\frac{1}{4}$ teaspoon freshly ground black pepper; cook for 2 minutes until the nuts are golden. Brush the cobs with the mixture, then roll in $\frac{3}{4}$ cup (80g) finely grated Parmesan combined with $\frac{1}{4}$ cup (10g) finely chopped flat-leaf parsley.

Moroccan lamb pilaf

HIGH-PROTEIN/FAST | PREP + COOK TIME **30 MINUTES** | SERVES **4**

PER SERVING | Energy kcals 618 | Carbohydrate 63g of which sugar 9g | Fat 26g of which saturates 7g | Salt 0.4g | Fibre 11g

Bulgur is wholegrain wheat parboiled and cracked into different grades of fineness. Whole grains contain all three parts of the grain kernel: the bran, germ, and endosperm. There is strong evidence that eating whole grains is good for us, reducing our risk of chronic diseases.

2 tbsp extra virgin olive oil

1 large onion (200g), thinly sliced

250g lean lamb mince

2 tbsp harissa seasoning, plus extra, to serve (optional)

$1/2$ bunch of coriander, leaves reserved, stems finely chopped

$1^1/_2$ cups (240g) coarse bulgur wheat, rinsed well

400g can chickpeas, drained, rinsed

2 carrots (240g), julienned

$1/4$ cup (20g) natural flaked almonds, toasted

$1/3$ cup (95g) Greek-style yogurt

1 Heat the olive oil in a large, heavy-based saucepan over a medium-high heat; cook the onion for 8 minutes or until golden brown and slightly crispy. Increase the heat to high; cook the lamb, breaking up any lumps with a wooden spoon, for 5 minutes or until well browned.

2 Add the harissa seasoning and chopped coriander stems; cook, stirring, for 1 minute or until fragrant. Add the bulgur wheat; cook, stirring, for 1 minute or until toasted. Add the chickpeas and $1^1/_2$ cups (375ml) water; bring to the boil. Reduce the heat to low; cook, covered, for 15 minutes or until the liquid has been absorbed. Remove from the heat; allow to stand, covered, for 5 minutes.

3 Fluff up the bulgur grains with a fork. Top the pilaf with the carrots, reserved coriander leaves, and almonds. Serve with the yogurt, dusted with extra harissa seasoning, if you like.

Harissa fish fingers with mushy peas

HIGH-PROTEIN | PREP + COOK TIME **35 MINUTES** | SERVES **4**

PER SERVING | Energy kcals 905 | Carbohydrate 57g of which sugar 8g | Fat 49g of which saturates 13g | Salt 0.9g plus seasoning | Fibre 10g

We've given classic fish fingers a healthier makeover using salmon and wholegrain bread
for crumbing, and replaced traditional mayonnaise with a tangy yogurt harissa sauce for
spooning over or alongside the fish fingers.

extra virgin olive oil cooking spray

2 large potatoes (600g), chopped

2¹/₂ cups (300g) frozen garden peas

¹/₄ cup (60ml) extra virgin olive oil

¹/₂ cup (10g) mint leaves, coarsely chopped, plus extra
sprigs, to serve

700g (1¹/₂lb) skinless tail-end salmon fillets

1¹/₄ cups (350g) Greek-style yogurt

1¹/₂ tbsp harissa paste

1 tbsp finely chopped drained cornichons

1 tbsp baby capers, finely chopped

4 slices of stale wholegrain bread (160g),
torn into chunks

salt and freshly ground black pepper

lemon wedges, to serve

1 Preheat the oven to 220°C (200°C fan/425°F/Gas 7). Place a large wire
rack over a large baking tray; spray the rack with extra virgin olive oil.

2 Put the chopped potatoes in a medium saucepan of cold water over a
high heat. Bring to the boil; cook for 20 minutes, adding the peas during
the last 1 minute of cooking time. Drain; allow the vegetables to stand
in the colander for 2 minutes to drain well. Return to the saucepan. Using
a potato masher, crush the potato and peas with the extra virgin olive oil
and mint. Season with salt and pepper to taste; cover to keep warm.

3 Cut the fish into 16 even finger-shaped pieces, about 3cm x 12cm.
Place the fish fingers in a large bowl.

4 Combine the yogurt and harissa in a medium bowl; season with salt and
pepper to taste. Add a heaped ¹/₃ cup of the yogurt mixture to the fish;
toss to coat evenly. Stir the cornichons and capers through the
remaining yogurt mixture; refrigerate the sauce until needed.

5 Process the bread until coarse crumbs form. Scatter the crumbs evenly
over the fish; press down on the crumbs to secure to the fish. (As the
crumbs are chunky, they may not completely coat the fish.) Arrange the
fish fingers on the prepared rack in a single layer. Spray generously with
extra virgin olive oil.

6 Bake the fish fingers for 12 minutes or until the crumbs are golden and
crisp, and the fish is cooked through. Serve immediately with the mushy
peas, harissa yogurt sauce, extra mint sprigs, and lemon wedges for
squeezing over.

TIP

Some fishmongers and supermarkets sell tail ends
separately. If unavailable, cut thick centre-cut
salmon fillets in half horizontally, then continue
as instructed in step 3.

Stovetop green chilli eggs with paneer

VEGETARIAN | PREP + COOK TIME **45 MINUTES** | SERVES **4**

PER SERVING | Energy kcals 676 | Carbohydrate 43g of which sugar 5g | Fat 37g of which saturates 13g | Salt 0.8g plus seasoning | Fibre 5g

A serving of 2 large eggs provides 580kJ of energy, 12.7g of protein, 10.3g of fat, and 1.4g of carbohydrate. Of the fat, less than a third is saturated fat and more than half is healthy monounsaturated fat – the same family of fats found in olive oil and avocados.

4 Desiree potatoes (800g), cut into 1cm slices

2½ tbsp extra virgin olive oil

2 tbsp curry leaves

1 large onion (200g), thinly sliced

2 long green chillies, seeded, finely chopped

½ cup (20g) finely chopped coriander leaves and stems

2 tsp garam masala

1 tsp cumin seeds

½ tsp ground turmeric

12 eggs

60g baby spinach leaves

200g paneer, crumbled

salt and freshly ground black pepper

1 Bring a large saucepan of water to the boil; add the sliced potatoes and cook for 8 minutes or until just tender. (Do not overcook the potato or it will break up with the second cooking in the frying pan.) Drain well.

2 Heat 2 tablespoons of the olive oil in a 25cm (base measurement) frying pan over a high heat. Add the curry leaves; cook for 1 minute or until crisp. Remove; drain on kitchen paper. Cook the onion in the same pan for 4 minutes or until softened. Add the chillies, chopped coriander, and spices; cook for a further 30 seconds. Remove from the pan.

3 Whisk 8 of the eggs in a large bowl. Arrange the sliced potato in the pan. Top with the onion mixture, half of the curry leaves, and the spinach. Pour over the beaten egg. Season with salt and pepper to taste. Make 4 indentations in the top of the egg mixture; crack the remaining eggs into each hole, and scatter with the paneer. Season with salt and pepper to taste.

4 Cover the frying pan with a tight-fitting lid. Cook over a low heat for 20 minutes or until the eggs are set and cooked to your liking. Serve immediately, topped with the remaining curry leaves and olive oil.

TIP

If you like your egg yolks soft, add the 4 remaining, unwhisked eggs halfway through the cooking time.

Speedy white bean and pea pasta

FAST/GLUTEN-FREE/HIGH-FIBRE | PREP + COOK TIME **20 MINUTES** | SERVES **4**

PER SERVING | Energy kcals 575 | Carbohydrate 66g of which sugar 7g | Fat 21g of which saturates 7g | Salt 0.3g plus seasoning | Fibre 12g

Peas, beans, and legumes are good sources of fibre, protein, and carbohydrate, as well as B vitamins and essential minerals such as iron, magnesium, and zinc. Regular intake may also lower blood pressure and cholesterol levels, and even help with weight control. Who knew that such a humble food group could have such a powerful effect on health?

250g gluten-free spaghetti

¼ cup (60ml) extra virgin olive oil

1 onion (150g), finely chopped

2 garlic cloves, crushed

400g can cannellini beans, drained, rinsed

2 cups (240g) frozen garden peas

¾ cup (180g) light soured cream

1 lemon (140g)

¾ cup (60g) finely grated Parmesan

¼ cup (10g) finely chopped fresh dill, plus extra dill sprigs, to serve

salt and freshly ground black pepper

1 Cook the spaghetti in a large saucepan of boiling salted water for 8 minutes or until almost tender. Drain, reserving ¾ cup (180ml) of the cooking water.

2 Meanwhile, heat 2 tablespoons of the olive oil in a large non-stick, heavy-based frying pan over a medium heat. Cook the onion and garlic, covered, stirring occasionally, for 5 minutes until soft.

3 Add the white beans, peas, and soured cream; reduce the heat to low. Cook for 1 minute. Using a potato masher, crush the beans and peas over a low heat until half of them are mashed; this will help to thicken the sauce. Cut the lemon in half. Juice one half; cut the remaining half into wedges. Add the Parmesan, chopped dill, and 1 tablespoon of the lemon juice to the bean mixture; season with salt and pepper to taste.

4 Add the hot pasta and reserved cooking water to the pan; cook, stirring, for 1 minute or until the pasta is coated in the sauce. Drizzle with the remaining olive oil and scatter with the extra dill sprigs. Serve immediately with the lemon wedges for squeezing over.

Mushroom tofu burger in butternut 'bun'

VEGETARIAN/HIGH-PROTEIN | PREP + COOK TIME **55 MINUTES + REFRIGERATION** | SERVES **4**
PER SERVING | Energy kcals 783 | Carbohydrate 93g of which sugar 38g | Fat 30g of which saturates 8g | Salt 2g plus seasoning | Fibre 13g

Tofu is a great source of amino acids, iron, and calcium. It is super-versatile, too, making it a great meat-substitute in the burgers here; nutritionally empty white burger buns are replaced by butternut squash for a veg-rich meal.

6 spring onions

300g extra-firm tofu, coarsely chopped

200g button mushrooms, coarsely chopped

2 garlic cloves, crushed

2 tbsp Dijon mustard

2 cups (200g) fresh wholegrain breadcrumbs

1 egg

2kg butternut squash, unpeeled

1/4 cup (60ml) extra virgin olive oil

4 slices of Swiss cheese (90g)

1 baby cos lettuce (90g), leaves separated

1 large vine-ripened tomato (220g), thinly sliced

1/4 cup (160g) tomato chutney

1 tsp sesame seeds, toasted

salt and freshly ground black pepper

1. Finely chop half of the spring onions. Process the chopped spring onions with the tofu, mushrooms, garlic, Dijon mustard, breadcrumbs, egg, and salt and pepper to taste until the mixture comes together. Shape the mixture into 4 patties; cover and refrigerate for 20 minutes to firm.

2. Meanwhile, cut the unpeeled butternut squash in half widthways; reserve the stem end for another use. Cut the remaining squash into eight 1cm rounds.

3. Heat 1 tablespoon of the olive oil in a large frying pan over a medium heat; cook half of the squash slices for 5 minutes on each side or until golden and cooked through. Drain on kitchen paper. Repeat with another 1 tablespoon of the olive oil and the remaining squash slices.

4. Cut the remaining spring onions into 12cm lengths, then slice these lengths into thin shreds. Place in a bowl of iced water to curl. Set aside; drain before using.

5. Heat the remaining olive oil in the same frying pan over a medium heat; cook the tofu patties for 2 minutes; turn over and cook for 1 minute. Top the patties with the cheese, and cook for a further minute or until golden and the cheese is starting to melt.

6. To assemble the burgers, place a squash round on each of 4 serving plates; top each one with the lettuce, a tofu patty, tomato slices, chutney, and some of the drained curled spring onion. Sandwich each stack with one of the remaining squash slices; secure with short skewers. Scatter with the toasted sesame seeds.

TIP

Roast the leftover squash to use in salads or turn into butternut squash soup.

Sweet potato and crumbed fish tray bake

ONE-PAN | PREP + COOK TIME **35 MINUTES** | SERVES **4**

PER SERVING | Energy kcals 640 | Carbohydrate 69g of which sugar 23g | Fat 16g of which saturates 5g | Salt 1g plus seasoning | Fibre 13g

White fish is an excellent source of iodine. A 100g portion, for example, provides you with more than a quarter of your daily requirements. Iodized salt (used to supplement dietary iodine) is not common in the UK and so iodine deficiency has re-emerged. Iodine is essential for the production of thyroid hormones that control metabolism.

extra virgin olive oil cooking spray

1kg orange sweet potato, cut into 2cm pieces

400g cherry vine tomatoes

250g snow peas (mangetout), trimmed

1/2 cup (40g) flaked almonds

3/4 cup (15g) flat-leaf parsley leaves, plus extra sprigs, to garnish (optional)

1 slice of stale wholegrain sourdough bread (80g), well toasted, coarsely torn

4 x 200g skinless firm white fish fillets

1/3 cup (95g) Greek-style yogurt

salt and freshly ground black pepper

1 lemon (140g), cut into wedges

cocktail sauce

1/2 cup (140g) Greek-style yogurt

2 tbsp lemon juice

2 tsp horseradish cream

extra virgin olive oil, to serve (optional)

1 Preheat the oven to 220°C (200°C fan/425°F/Gas 7). Lightly oil a wire rack with extra virgin olive oil cooking spray; place over a baking tray. Line a second large baking tray with baking parchment.

2 Reserve 3/4 cup of the sweet potato for the crumb; spread the remaining sweet potato over the lined baking tray. Spray with the olive oil; season with salt and pepper to taste. Bake the sweet potato for 20 minutes or until golden. Reserve 2 tomatoes for the cocktail sauce; add the remaining tomatoes and snow peas to the tray. Spray with the olive oil; bake for a further 5 minutes.

3 Meanwhile, put the reserved sweet potato in a food processor with the almonds, 1/2 cup of the parsley leaves, and the toasted bread. Process to form coarse crumbs. Put in a medium bowl; season well with salt and a good grinding of pepper.

4 Place the fish on the prepared oiled rack. Using the back of a spoon, spread 1 tablespoon yogurt evenly over the top of each fish fillet. Press on the crumb mixture; spray with the olive oil. Bake for 12 minutes or until the crumb is golden and the fish is cooked through.

5 Meanwhile, to make the cocktail sauce, finely grate the reserved cherry tomatoes from step 2; place in a bowl with the yogurt, lemon juice, and horseradish cream. Mix well to combine; season with salt and pepper to taste. Drizzle with a little extra virgin olive oil, if you like.

6 Toss the remaining parsley leaves through the roast vegetables; top with the fish. Serve with the cocktail sauce, lemon wedges for squeezing over, and extra parsley sprigs, if you like.

Cauliflower and tofu curry

VEGETARIAN | PREP + COOK TIME **35 MINUTES** | SERVES **4**

PER SERVING | Energy kcals 632 | Carbohydrate 29g of which sugar 13g | Fat 42g of which saturates 21g | Salt 0.3g plus seasoning | Fibre 12g

A plant-based curry is an easy way to increase your vegetable intake. Each of the vegetables here offers a unique array of nutrients. Garlic and shallots contain prebiotics called fructo-oligosaccharides (FOS), which when included in our diet promote the growth of healthy bacteria in the gut. This recipe does have a high amount of saturated fat, though, so make sure to reserve this dish for an otherwise lean day.

2 x 4cm piece of fresh root ginger (40g)

¼ cup (60ml) extra virgin olive oil

8 shallots, halved

2 tbsp curry powder

1 tsp ground turmeric

400ml can light coconut cream

1 cup (250ml) vegetable stock

½ large cauliflower (1kg), cut into large florets

450g firm tofu, cut into 2.5cm pieces

1¼ cups (150g) frozen garden peas

⅓ cup (3g) curry leaves

2 garlic cloves, thinly sliced

salt and freshly ground black pepper

steamed brown rice, to serve

lime wedges, to serve

1 Peel the ginger; finely grate 1 piece of the ginger and thinly slice the remaining piece. Heat 1 tablespoon of the olive oil in a large, heavy-based saucepan over a medium heat; cook the shallots, covered, for 2 minutes or until starting to soften and the edges are turning golden.

2 Add the curry powder, turmeric, and grated ginger; cook, stirring, for 30 seconds until fragrant. Add the coconut cream and vegetable stock; cook, scraping the bottom of the pan with a wooden spoon, until well combined. Add the cauliflower and tofu; cook, covered, for 15 minutes or until the cauliflower is just tender, stirring halfway through the cooking time. Add the peas for the last 2 minutes of cooking time. Season with salt and pepper to taste.

3 Meanwhile, heat the remaining olive oil in a small, heavy-based saucepan over a medium heat. Taking care as the oil will splutter, add the sliced ginger, curry leaves, and garlic. Cook, stirring frequently, for 2 minutes or until the curry leaves are crisp. Stir half of the ginger mixture through the curry.

4 Top the curry with the remaining ginger mixture. Serve with steamed brown rice and lime wedges for squeezing over.

Vietnamese-style aubergine noodles

FAST | PREP + COOK TIME **30 MINUTES** | SERVES **4**

PER SERVING | Energy kcals 365 | Carbohydrate 60g of which sugar 17g | Fat 6g of which saturates 1g | Salt 2.9g | Fibre 8g

To make this bold and vibrantly coloured Vietnamese-inspired recipe vegetarian, swap the fish sauce with the same amount of dark soy sauce. Make sure you eat the noodles with a generous handful of herbs for the added freshness typical of Vietnamese cuisine.

1 large aubergine (500g), cut into 2cm pieces

200g fresh shiitake mushrooms, thinly sliced

2 shallots (50g), thinly sliced

1 tbsp fish sauce

1 tbsp runny honey

1 tbsp extra virgin olive oil

1$\frac{1}{2}$ tsp Chinese five-spice

200g dried brown rice vermicelli noodles

250g green beans, trimmed, halved lengthways

extra virgin olive oil cooking spray

4 small rice paper rounds (40g)

2 tsp black sesame seeds

2 carrots (240g), peeled, julienned

$\frac{1}{2}$ bunch of mint leaves, sprigs picked

nuoc cham

2 tbsp fish sauce

2$\frac{1}{2}$ tbsp white vinegar

1$\frac{1}{2}$ tbsp runny honey or coconut sugar

1 small red chilli, finely chopped (optional)

1 Preheat the oven to 200°C (180°C fan/400°F/Gas 6). Line a baking tray with baking parchment.

2 Put the aubergine, mushrooms, half of the sliced shallots, fish sauce, honey, olive oil, and Chinese five-spice in a large bowl; mix well to coat. Spread the vegetable mixture over the prepared tray; roast for 20 minutes, stirring halfway through the cooking time, or until the vegetables are golden brown.

3 Meanwhile, place the noodles and beans in a large heatproof bowl; cover with boiling water. Allow to stand for 5 minutes or until the noodles are soft. Drain and rinse under cold running water.

4 To make the nuoc cham, put the ingredients in a small saucepan; add $\frac{1}{2}$ cup (125ml) water. Stir over a low heat until the honey dissolves and the mixture almost reaches a simmer. Set aside to keep warm.

5 Spray 1 rice paper round with the extra virgin olive oil cooking spray; sprinkle with $\frac{1}{2}$ teaspoon of the sesame seeds. Microwave on HIGH (100%) for 50 seconds or until puffed up and white. Repeat with the remaining rice papers and sesame seeds.

6 Divide the noodles, carrots, green beans, and aubergine mixture among 4 serving bowls; top with the mint sprigs and remaining shallots. Pour over the hot nuoc cham. Serve with the rice paper crackers.

Green curry steamed fish parcels

HIGH-PROTEIN/FAST | PREP + COOK TIME **30 MINUTES** | SERVES **4**

PER SERVING | Energy kcals 397 | Carbohydrate 28g of which sugar 8g | Fat 16g of which saturates 11g | Salt 3.3g plus seasoning | Fibre 3g

Cooking fish in a paper parcel is a beautifully healthy way of preparing it. The aromatic cooking liquid flavours the fish while creating steam to cook it. This is a particularly good method for delicate white fish, which can fall apart with direct-heat cooking methods.

100g dried brown rice vermicelli noodles

¼ cup (75g) Thai green curry paste

270ml can coconut milk

2 tbsp fish sauce

1 tbsp light soft brown sugar

500g Asian greens such as pak choi, choy sum, or tatsoi, cut into thirds

4 x 150g boneless firm white fish fillets (600g), skin on

6 makrut lime leaves

½ cup (15g) Thai basil leaves, plus extra, to serve

1 long green chilli, thinly sliced

lime wedges, to serve

1 Put the noodles in a heatproof bowl; cover with boiling water. Allow to stand for 5 minutes until soft; drain well.

2 Mix together the curry paste, coconut milk, fish sauce, and brown sugar in a small jug.

3 Place four 50cm lengths of foil on a work surface. Top each one with a sheet of baking parchment half the size, placed at one end of the foil.

4 Divide the Asian greens, fish, and 4 of the makrut lime leaves among each piece of baking parchment, positioning in the centre. Slowly pour one-quarter of the green curry mixture over each piece of fish and top with the basil leaves. Bring the foil up and over the filling, fold the edges to seal and form a half-moon shape.

5 Place the parcels in a large bamboo steamer over a wok of simmering water; cover with a lid. Steam the parcels for 15 minutes or until the fish is cooked through.

6 Shred the remaining lime leaves. Carefully open the parcels; add the drained noodles. Serve immediately, scattered with the chilli, extra Thai basil leaves, shredded lime leaves, and lime wedges for squeezing over.

TIP

If you don't have a large bamboo steamer, preheat the oven to 180°C (160°C fan/350°F/Gas 4). Place the parcels on a large baking tray; bake for 20 minutes.

Oven-baked gluten-free crumbed chicken with pea purée

GLUTEN-FREE/HIGH-FIBRE | PREP **35 MINUTES** | SERVES **4**

PER SERVING | Energy kcals 518 | Carbohydrate 24g of which sugar 7g | Fat 21g of which saturates 4g | Salt 0.4g plus seasoning | Fibre 8g

Quinoa and almonds are both used to make the nutritious crumbing for the chicken. Quinoa is rich in several B group vitamins required to turn the food you eat into energy to fuel your body, while almonds are head and shoulders above other nuts for vitamin E.

extra virgin olive oil cooking spray

$^2/_3$ cup (55g) quinoa flakes

$^1/_3$ cup (55g) natural almonds, finely chopped

$^1/_3$ cup (25g) finely grated Parmesan

1 egg, lightly beaten

2 x 300g skinless boneless chicken breasts, halved lengthways

300g mixed cherry vine tomatoes

4 cups (480g) frozen garden peas, thawed

2 cups (60g) basil leaves

2 tbsp extra virgin olive oil

sea salt and freshly ground black pepper

1 small lemon (65g), cut into wedges, to serve

1 Preheat the oven to 220°C (200°C fan/425°F/Gas 7). Line a baking tray with baking parchment. Top with a wire rack; spray the rack with extra virgin olive oil.

2 Put the quinoa, almonds, and Parmesan in a shallow tray; stir through to mix evenly. Season well with sea salt and a good grinding of pepper. Put the beaten egg in a shallow bowl. Dip the chicken into the egg, then press into the quinoa crumbs to coat.

3 Place the chicken on the rack on the prepared tray; spray with the olive oil. Bake, turning halfway through the cooking time, for 20 minutes. Add the tomatoes to the tray; bake for a further 5 minutes or until the tomatoes are blistered and the chicken is golden brown.

4 Meanwhile, process the peas, $1^1/_2$ cups (45g) of the basil, and the olive oil, scraping down the sides, for 2 minutes or until smooth. Season with salt and pepper to taste.

5 Serve the chicken with the pea purée, blistered tomatoes, and lemon wedges for squeezing over; top with the remaining basil leaves.

FEEDING
A CROWD

Looking for inspiration for a celebration
feast or leisurely lunch? Or wondering how
to feed any unexpected extras at the dinner
table? These recipes will have you covered.

Smoky red lentil 'meat-less' loaf

VEGETARIAN | PREP + COOK TIME **1 HOUR 20 MINUTES + OVERNIGHT STANDING** | SERVES **4**
PER SERVING | Energy kcals 734 | Carbohydrate 72g of which sugar 29g | Fat 31g of which saturates 13g | Salt 1.9g plus seasoning | Fibre 13g

This plant-based loaf has the heartiness of a meatloaf without the meat, making it a filling meal for those days you need comfort food. Leftovers can be toasted in a sandwich press and served piled onto wholemeal bread, with salad leaves and a little tomato relish.

You will need to soak the lentils 8 hours ahead

1¼ cups (250g) dried red lentils

2 tbsp extra virgin olive oil, plus extra for greasing

1 onion (150g), finely chopped

2 garlic cloves, finely chopped

¼ cup (3g) oregano leaves, finely chopped

1 tsp smoked paprika

1 carrot (120g)

2 parsnips (500g)

3 eggs, lightly beaten

½ cup (125ml) vegetable stock

1½ cups (180g) grated Cheddar

salt and freshly ground black pepper

120g mixed salad leaves, to serve

1 cup (275g) tomato and smoky chipotle relish, to serve

1 Put the lentils in a large bowl; cover with cold water. Allow to stand for 8 hours or overnight. Drain; rinse under cold water, then drain well.

2 Preheat the oven to 200°C (180°C fan/400°F/Gas 6). Oil a 13cm x 23cm x 6cm loaf tin; line the bottom and sides with baking parchment.

3 Heat the olive oil in a medium frying pan over a medium heat. Cook the onion, garlic, and oregano, stirring occasionally, for 5 minutes or until softened. Stir in the paprika. Set aside to cool.

4 Meanwhile, scrub the carrot and parsnips; leave unpeeled. Thinly slice half of 1 parsnip lengthways. Coarsely grate the remaining parsnip and the carrot. Combine the grated vegetables, beaten eggs, vegetable stock, 1¼ cups of the Cheddar, lentils, and onion mixture in a large bowl; season with salt and pepper to taste. Spoon the mixture into the prepared tin; spread and level the mixture using the back of a spoon. Top with the sliced parsnip; sprinkle over the remaining Cheddar. Cover with foil greased with a little olive oil. Scrunch the foil around the sides of the tin to secure.

5 Bake the loaf for 30 minutes. Remove the foil; bake for a further 30 minutes or until golden.

6 Leave the loaf in the tin to stand for 5 minutes before turning, top-side up, onto a board. Cool for 15 minutes before slicing. Serve with the salad leaves and tomato and smoky chipotle relish.

TIP

You can pan-fry slices of the lentil loaf to serve in a burger bun, for a vegetarian burger patty.

Black barley pilaf and roasted sweet potato

VEGETARIAN | PREP + COOK TIME **1 HOUR 30 MINUTES** | SERVES **6**

PER SERVING | Energy kcals 663 | Carbohydrate 95g of which sugar 22g | Fat 23g of which saturates 6g | Salt 0.9g plus seasoning | Fibre 11g

Black barley has the bran layer intact, and is super nutritious with a chewy, pleasant texture and a nutty taste. The dark pigment anthocyanin is the same as that found in blueberries and other dark purple or black foods. These are known to have anti-inflammatory properties.

6 orange sweet potatoes (1.8kg)

1/3 cup (80ml) extra virgin olive oil

1 onion (150g), finely chopped

1 tbsp ground cumin

1 cup (200g) black barley (see tip)

2 cups (500ml) vegetable stock

1/4 cup (35g) dried sweetened cranberries, chopped

1/2 cup (15g) coarsely chopped flat-leaf parsley, plus extra 1/3 cup (10g) firmly packed flat-leaf parsley leaves, to serve

1/2 cup (90g) pistachios, chopped

125g soft Danish or Persian-style feta, crumbled

salt and freshly ground black pepper

1 Preheat the oven to 180°C (160°C fan/350°F/Gas 4). Line a baking tray with baking parchment.

2 Scrub the sweet potatoes; leave unpeeled, but cut in half lengthways. Arrange the sweet potatoes, cut-side up, on the prepared tray; drizzle with 2 tablespoons of the olive oil; season with salt and pepper to taste. Bake for 1 hour or until tender.

3 Meanwhile, heat 1 tablespoon of the olive oil in a large saucepan over a medium heat. Add the onion; cook, stirring occasionally, for 5 minutes or until the onion softens. Add the cumin; stir for 30 seconds until fragrant. Add the barley; stir to mix through evenly. Add the stock; bring to the boil. Reduce the heat to low; cook, covered, for 40 minutes or until almost all the liquid has been absorbed and the barley is tender. Remove from the heat; stir in the cranberries and chopped parsley.

4 Remove the flesh in the centre of the sweet potatoes with a spoon, leaving a 1cm shell. Cut the scooped flesh into pieces.

5 Spoon the pilaf mixture into the sweet potato shells, mounding it slightly. Top with the sweet potato pieces, pistachios, and crumbled feta. Bake for 10 minutes or until the filling is heated through and the feta is a light golden colour.

6 Serve the sweet potatoes drizzled with the remaining olive oil and topped with the extra parsley leaves.

TIP

If black barley is unavailable, substitute with regular barley or farro.

Mushroom and sweetcorn soft tacos

HEALTHY FATS | PREP + COOK TIME **40 MINUTES** | SERVES **4**
PER SERVING | Energy kcals 633 | Carbohydrate 41g of which sugar 11g | Fat 38g of which saturates 9g | Salt 2.2g plus seasoning | Fibre 11g

Mushrooms are rich in B vitamins and fibre, while the cottage cheese and black bean salsa
contribute protein. Avocados are a surprisingly good source of vitamin C. This makes them
a great addition to a vegetarian meal, as they will help you to absorb more plant iron.

300g firm tofu, drained

3 large portobello mushrooms (600g), chopped

200g chestnut mushrooms, halved

200g small button mushrooms

1¼ cups (320g) black bean and chipotle salsa (see tip)

½ bunch of coriander (45g), leaves reserved, stems
and roots finely chopped

2 tbsp extra virgin olive oil, plus extra for drizzling
(optional)

1 trimmed cob of sweetcorn (250g), kernels removed

8 small white corn or flour tortillas (200g)

250g cottage cheese

1 large avocado (320g)

120g cherry tomatoes, quartered

salt and freshly ground black pepper

1 Crumble the tofu into a large bowl, forming a mixture of large and small
chunks. Add the mushrooms, salsa, and 2 tablespoons of the chopped
coriander stems and roots; stir well to mix evenly.

2 Heat 1 tablespoon of the olive oil in a large, heavy-based non-stick frying
pan over a high heat. Add half of the mushroom mixture; cook, stirring
occasionally, for 8 minutes or until the mushrooms are browned and
tender. Transfer to a bowl. Repeat with the remaining 1 tablespoon olive
oil and the mushroom mixture. Return all the mushrooms to the pan with
the sweetcorn; stir to mix through. Season with salt and pepper to taste.
Remove the pan from the heat; cover to keep warm.

3 Meanwhile, preheat a ridged cast-iron grill pan to a medium heat.
Cook the tortillas, one at a time, for 30 seconds on each side or until
grill marks appear. Transfer to a plate; keep warm.

4 Process the cottage cheese and avocado until smooth. Season with salt
and pepper to taste.

5 Stir ½ cup of the reserved coriander leaves through the mushroom
mixture; divide evenly among the tortillas. Top with the tomatoes and
remaining coriander leaves. Serve the tacos with the avocado-cottage
cheese, drizzled with extra olive oil, if you like.

TIPS

- If you like things spicy, add a pinch of dried chilli
flakes or sliced fresh chilli to the mushrooms.
- If you can't find black bean and chipotle salsa,
make your own chunky salsa by mixing a smoky
chipotle salsa with some drained black beans.

Oven-baked veggie sesame tempura with soba noodles

VEGETARIAN | PREP + COOK TIME **25 MINUTES** | SERVES **4**

PER SERVING | Energy kcals 652 | Carbohydrate 93g of which sugar 14g | Fat 19g of which saturates 3g | Salt 3.6g plus seasoning | Fibre 9g

Soba noodles are a low-GI Japanese noodle made from a mixture of buckwheat and wheat, making them both high in dietary fibre and a complete protein. Sodium content is high; however, this is reduced significantly after cooking.

270g buckwheat soba noodles

1 tbsp sesame oil

$1/2$ cup (80g) toasted sesame seeds, crushed, plus extra 1 tbsp

$2/3$ cup (120g) rice flour

2 tsp sea salt flakes

5 egg whites, lightly whisked until frothy

175g broccolini (Tenderstem broccoli), trimmed, blanched (see tip)

150g oyster mushrooms

300g butternut squash, skin on, thinly sliced

ginger dressing

$1^1/2$ tbsp tamari

$1/3$ cup (80ml) mirin

$1/4$ cup (70g) pink pickled ginger, plus 2 tbsp of the pickling liquid

1 tsp sesame oil

1 baby cucumber (30g), finely chopped

1 spring onion, thinly sliced

salt and freshly ground black pepper

1 Cook the noodles in a large saucepan of boiling water for 3 minutes or until just tender. Drain and refresh under cold running water until cool; toss with the sesame oil. Set aside.

2 Preheat the oven to 220°C (200°C fan/425°F/Gas 7). Line 2 large baking trays with baking parchment.

3 Put the sesame seeds, rice flour, and sea salt flakes in a shallow bowl; stir through. Put the whisked egg whites in a second shallow bowl.

4 Working in batches, dip the broccolini, mushrooms, and pumpkin into the egg white, then into the flour mixture, shaking to remove any excess. Place on the prepared trays. Bake, turning halfway through during the cooking time, for 10 minutes or until the vegetables are crisp and golden.

5 Meanwhile, to make the ginger dressing, put the tamari, mirin, pickling liquid, and sesame oil in a screw-top jar with a tight-fitting lid; shake well. Season with salt and pepper to taste. Transfer to a small bowl; stir in the cucumber, spring onion, and pickled ginger.

6 Arrange the noodles on each of 4 serving plates. Drizzle half of the dressing over the noodles. Top with the tempura vegetables. Serve with the remaining dressing, sprinkled with the extra 1 tablespoon sesame seeds.

TIP

To blanch the broccolini (Tenderstem broccoli), place in a heatproof bowl; pour over boiling water. Stand until bright green. Drain; then refresh under cold running water. Pat dry with kitchen paper.

Chicken, broccoli pesto, and pulse pasta

HIGH-PROTEIN | PREP + COOK TIME **30 MINUTES** | SERVES **4**

PER SERVING | Energy kcals 753 | Carbohydrate 72g of which sugar 4g | Fat 29g of which saturates 6g | Salt 0.4g plus seasoning | Fibre 9g

Pulse pastas are a terrific way to boost your intake of plant-based food. Depending on the brand and shape, this type of pasta is made from a variety of different pulses such as chickpeas and lentils. The benefit is a more filling and nutritious pasta.

2 skinless boneless chicken breasts (400g)

375g dried chickpea or lentil pasta such as penne

300g broccoli, coarsely chopped

1 cup (50g) firmly packed basil leaves, plus extra, to serve

1/2 cup (70g) pistachios, roasted

1 garlic clove, crushed

1/2 cup (40g) finely grated Parmesan

1/3 cup (80ml) extra virgin olive oil

1/3 cup (80ml) lemon juice

1 tsp finely grated lemon zest

2 cups (70g) shredded curly kale

salt and freshly ground black pepper

1 lemon (140g), cut into wedges, to serve

1 Put the chicken in a deep frying pan; cover with cold water. Bring to the boil, then reduce the heat to a gentle simmer; poach for 10 minutes or until cooked through. Allow to cool; coarsely shred.

2 Meanwhile, cook the pasta in a large saucepan of salted boiling water for 6 minutes or until almost tender; drain. Return the pasta to the pan.

3 At the same time, process the broccoli, basil, pistachios, garlic, Parmesan, olive oil, lemon juice, and lemon zest until smooth. Season with salt and pepper to taste.

4 Combine the chicken, kale, and pesto with the pasta in the pan. Season with salt and pepper to taste; toss well. Scatter the pasta with extra basil leaves; serve with the lemon wedges for squeezing over.

Fish skewers with pepper and seed dressing

HIGH-PROTEIN | PREP + COOK TIME **35 MINUTES + REFRIGERATION** | SERVES **4**
PER SERVING | Energy kcals 478 | Carbohydrate 10g of which sugar 5g | Fat 23g of which saturates 4g | Salt 1.2g plus seasoning | Fibre 7g

While oily fish such as sardines, salmon, and mackerel often get all the kudos, and white fish
do not contain omega-3 fats, they do provide a wealth of other nutrients. They are protein-
rich, with a 100g fillet providing you with 20g of high-quality protein.

1 large bunch of coriander (150g)

1 cup (240g) chopped drained chargrilled peppers

2 tbsp chipotle in adobo sauce

2 garlic cloves, crushed

$^1/_2$ cup (75g) natural mixed seeds with
pine nuts, toasted

1 tsp ground cumin

2 tbsp extra virgin olive oil

1kg skinless firm white fish fillets, cut into
3cm pieces

1$^1/_2$ tbsp lemon juice

2 courgettes (240g), thinly sliced lengthways

salt and freshly ground black pepper

broccoli rice

1 large head of broccoli (400g), trimmed,
cut into florets

2 tbsp extra virgin olive oil

1 Wash the coriander well; pick the leaves and reserve. Chop the roots
and stems; you will need $^1/_3$ cup. Process the coriander roots and stems,
chargrilled peppers, chipotle, garlic, seed mix, cumin, and olive oil until
they form a paste. Season with salt and pepper to taste.

2 Put the fish in a large bowl, and add half of the pepper paste; toss to coat.
Cover and refrigerate for 10 minutes. Stir the lemon juice through the
remaining pepper paste to form the dressing; set aside.

3 Meanwhile, to make the broccoli rice, pulse the broccoli in a food
processor until it resembles grains of rice. Heat the olive oil in a large
frying pan over a medium heat; cook the broccoli for 2 minutes or until
bright green and softened slightly. Stir through $^3/_4$ cup of the reserved
coriander leaves. Season with salt and pepper to taste.

4 Thread the fish onto 8 metal or soaked bamboo skewers alternately with
the courgette ribbons. Preheat an oiled ridged cast-iron grill pan to a
high heat; cook the skewers, turning, for 8 minutes or until just cooked
through and grill marks appear.

5 Serve the skewers with the broccoli rice, topped with the pepper and
seed dressing and the remaining reserved coriander leaves.

TIP

Slice the courgettes into ribbons with a vegetable
peeler, mandolin, or V-slicer. If using bamboo
skewers, soak them in boiling water for 10 minutes.

Prawn and sweet potato panang curry

HIGH-PROTEIN | PREP + COOK TIME **30 MINUTES** | SERVES **4**

PER SERVING | Energy kcals 539 | Carbohydrate 55g of which sugar 18g | Fat 21g of which saturates 8g | Salt 2.6g | Fibre 10g

For years people worried about the cholesterol found in prawns. Today, we understand much more about what dietary factors affect our blood cholesterol profile. Dietary cholesterol is a minor factor. If you have a poor cholesterol profile, concentrate on changing the types of fat in your diet rather than worrying about cholesterol in food.

¹/₄ cup (75g) Thai red curry paste

1 red onion (170g), thinly sliced

8cm piece of fresh root ginger (40g), grated

1 orange sweet potato (400g), cut into 1.5cm thick rounds

¹/₄ cup (70g) smooth peanut butter

400ml can light coconut milk

2 cups (500ml) vegetable stock

400g peeled uncooked prawns

350g snow peas (mangetout), cut into thirds

1 tbsp fish sauce

1 tbsp lime juice

1 tbsp pure maple syrup

¹/₂ cup (20g) firmly packed coriander leaves

2 spring onions, shredded

1. Put the curry paste, onion, and ginger in a large, heavy-based saucepan over a low heat. Cook, covered, stirring occasionally, for 10 minutes or until the onion is softened.

2. Increase the heat to medium; stir in the sweet potato, peanut butter, coconut milk, and vegetable stock until combined. Bring to a simmer; cook, covered, for 15 minutes or until a sharp knife can be inserted into the sweet potato without resistance.

3. Add the prawns and snow peas to the curry; cook, uncovered, for a further 3 minutes or until the prawns are just cooked through. Stir through the fish sauce, lime juice, maple syrup, and half of the coriander.

4. Serve the curry evenly divided among 4 serving bowls, topped with the shredded spring onions and the remaining coriander leaves.

TIP

Serve with steamed brown and wild rice and coarsely chopped salted roasted peanuts.

Quick inside-out roast chicken

HIGH-PROTEIN | PREP + COOK TIME **1 HOUR 5 MINUTES** | SERVES **4**

PER SERVING | Energy kcals 690 | Carbohydrate 41g of which sugar 15g | Fat 25g of which saturates 5g | Salt 2.1g plus seasoning | Fibre 11g

One of the quandaries of cooking a whole chicken is that the breast and leg meat require different cooking times. Add in a stuffing to the chicken and you further increase the chances of dry breast meat. Roasting the stuffing outside of the chicken solves the problem.

1 whole chicken (1.8kg)

1/2 cup (12g) firmly packed sage leaves

1/4 cup (60ml) extra virgin olive oil, plus extra 1 tsp

2 carrots (240g), trimmed

1 large onion (200g)

1 cup (90g) rolled oats

110g wholemeal bread

1/4 cup (35g) sultanas, chopped

1 tsp sea salt flakes

1 large lemon (200g), halved

400g green beans

1 tsp finely grated lemon zest

salt and freshly ground black pepper

1 Preheat the oven to 200°C (180°C fan/400°F/Gas 6).

2 Place the chicken, breast-side down, on a chopping board. Using a pair of kitchen scissors, cut down either side of the chicken backbone to remove it; reserve the backbone. Press down lightly on the chicken legs to open the chicken out flat. Using a large, sharp knife, cut down through the breastbone and skin onto the board to halve the chicken.

3 Place the chicken backbone in the centre of a 24cm x 32cm roasting pan; place the chicken, skin-side up, on top of the backbone. Rub with 1 tablespoon of the olive oil; season with salt and pepper to taste. Scatter with half of the sage leaves.

4 Process the carrots, onion, oats, bread, sultanas, and remaining sage and olive oil with the sea salt flakes until finely chopped and the mixture holds together when pressed. Divide the stuffing evenly into 8 large balls; arrange the stuffing and the lemon halves around the chicken in the roasting pan.

5 Bake the chicken and stuffing for 50 minutes or until the chicken is golden and cooked through. Allow the chicken to rest, loosely covered in foil, for 10 minutes.

6 Meanwhile, put the green beans on a baking tray; toss with the extra 1 teaspoon oil. Season with salt and pepper to taste. Cook on the top shelf of the oven for 10 minutes.

7 Serve the chicken with the stuffing, green beans, and lemon halves, sprinkled with the lemon zest.

TIP

If you like, line the roasting pan with a large piece of baking parchment before adding the chicken. This makes for an easier clean-up once the cooking is done.

Roast veggies

Roasting brings out the natural sweetness in vegetables – particularly root vegetables – heightening their flavour and transforming them into irresistible bundles of goodness for your taste buds. And all the while you still gain the benefits of their fibre and nutrients.

Parsnip and apple

PREP + COOK TIME **40 MINUTES** | SERVES **4**

Preheat the oven to 200°C (180°C fan/400°F/Gas 6). Scrub and trim 4 parsnips (1kg) and core 2 red eating apples (300g). Cut the parsnips and apples lengthways into wedges. Line a baking tray with baking parchment. Arrange the parsnips and apples on the tray. Drizzle with 2 tablespoons each of runny honey and extra virgin olive oil, then add 6 small sprigs of rosemary. Season with salt and freshly ground black pepper to taste; toss to coat. Roast for 30 minutes or until the parsnips and apples are tender and browned. Add 2 slices of torn prosciutto; roast for a further 5 minutes or until crisp.

Pumpkin and chickpeas

PREP + COOK TIME **45 MINUTES** | SERVES **4**

Preheat the oven to 220°C (200°C fan/425°F/Gas 7). Cut 1kg kabocha squash (Japanese pumpkin), with the skin on, and 2 red onions (340g) lengthways into wedges. Drain a 400g can chickpeas; rinse. Place the squash, onion, chickpeas, and 10 torn thyme sprigs on a baking tray lined with baking parchment. Drizzle with ¼ cup (60ml) extra virgin olive oil. Season with salt and freshly ground black pepper to taste; toss to coat. Roast for 40 minutes or until the squash is tender and browned. Serve tossed with rocket, if you like.

Beetroot and almond crumble

PREP + COOK TIME **1 HOUR** | SERVES **4**

Preheat the oven to 220°C (200°C fan/425°F/Gas 7). Trim the leaves and stalks from 1kg baby red beetroot and 500g baby yellow beetroot; wash. Peel the red beetroot; cut in half. Keep the yellow ones whole and unpeeled. Place each coloured beetroot on a large piece of foil on a baking tray. Add 2 bay leaves; drizzle with 1 tablespoon olive oil. Cover each with another piece of foil to make parcels; seal. Roast the red beetroot for 40 minutes and the yellow beetroot for 30 minutes or until tender. Carefully peel the yellow beetroot; halve if large. Process ½ cup (80g) roasted natural almonds and ¼ cup (5g) flat-leaf parsley until chopped. Sprinkle the roasted beetroot with the almond crumble.

Heirloom carrots

PREP + COOK TIME **40 MINUTES** | SERVES **6**

Preheat the oven to 200°C (180°C fan/400°F/Gas 6). Scrub 1 bunch each of orange, white, and purple heirloom carrots. Trim the stalks to 2cm long, reserving the carrot tops; you will need 1kg trimmed carrots. Pick 1 cup (20g) small, tender leaves from the reserved carrot tops; wash. Discard the remaining tops. Process the tops with ½ cup (125ml) extra virgin olive oil, ¼ cup (60ml) red wine vinegar, 1 tablespoon runny honey, and 2 teaspoons cumin seeds until finely chopped. Season with salt and freshly ground black pepper to taste. Drizzle half of the dressing over the carrots; roast for 30 minutes or until tender. Serve topped with the remaining dressing.

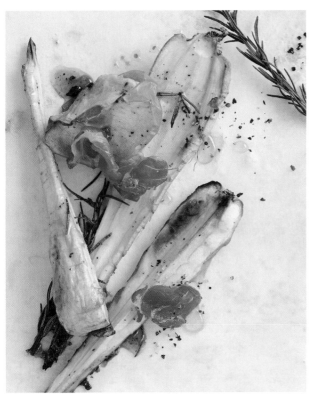

Cauliflower and chicken yogurt tandoori rice

GLUTEN-FREE | PREP + COOK TIME **40 MINUTES** | SERVES **4**

PER SERVING | Energy kcals 854 | Carbohydrate 60g of which sugar 15g | Fat 42g of which saturates 10g | Salt 1.9g plus seasoning | Fibre 11g

It is easy to single out individual ingredients and their attributes, but also important
for capturing maximum nutrients is eating from a wide array of food groups. Increasingly,
evidence is showing that it may be good for our gut health, too.

1 small cauliflower (800g)

600g chicken tenderloins (skinless mini
chicken fillets)

125g gluten-free tandoori paste

1 cup (280g) Greek-style yogurt

¼ cup (60ml) extra virgin olive oil

4 spring onions, cut into 3cm lengths

1 cup (200g) red quinoa

250g microwave or instant brown rice

2½ cups (625ml) vegetable stock

¼ cup (40g) unsalted cashews

1 cucumber (130g), thinly sliced into rounds

1 cup (30g) coriander leaves

salt and freshly ground black pepper

1 Preheat the oven to 220°C (200°C fan/425°F/Gas 7).

2 Cut the cauliflower into quarters, keeping the pale green leaves
attached. Trim off a little of the central core, but not too much because
you want to keep the florets attached; discard the core. Put the
cauliflower quarters and chicken in a large bowl; add the tandoori
paste and ½ cup (140g) of the yogurt; mix well until evenly coated.

3 Heat 2 tablespoons of the olive oil in a deep 30cm ovenproof frying pan
over a medium heat. Add the spring onions and quinoa; cook, stirring,
for 2 minutes or until the quinoa starts to crackle.

4 Add the rice and vegetable stock; lightly season with salt and pepper.
Arrange the chicken, then the cauliflower, over the quinoa mixture,
ensuring the cauliflower florets are on top and facing upwards.

5 Transfer the rice mixture to the oven; bake for 20 minutes. Reduce the
oven temperature to 200°C (180°C fan/400°F/Gas 6). Scatter over
the cashews; cook for a further 10 minutes or until the cauliflower
tops are golden and the stock has been absorbed.

6 Top with the sliced cucumber, coriander leaves, and remaining olive oil.
Serve with the remaining yogurt.

TIP

To make the recipe vegetarian, replace the
chicken with the same weight of firm tofu.

Turkish oven-roasted beans

VEGETARIAN/HIGH-FIBRE | PREP + COOK TIME **50 MINUTES** | SERVES **4**

PER SERVING | Energy kcals 816 | Carbohydrate 96g of which sugar 16g | Fat 24g of which saturates 11g | Salt 3.7g plus seasoning | Fibre 24g

Pomegranate molasses adds a sweet–sour flavour to this recipe. Also known as pomegranate syrup, its roots lie in Persian cuisine. If you don't have pomegranate molasses on hand, replace it with 2 teaspoons balsamic vinegar combined with 2 teaspoons pure maple syrup.

1 large fennel bulb (550g)

2 tbsp extra virgin olive oil

1 tsp ground allspice

2 tsp cumin seeds

400g can cherry tomatoes

2 x 400g cans butterbeans, drained, rinsed

2 tbsp pomegranate molasses

225g haloumi, sliced

1/4 cup (10g) firmly packed flat-leaf parsley leaves

salt and freshly ground black pepper

4 wholemeal pitta bread pockets (600g), halved, toasted, to serve

1. Preheat the oven to 220°C (200°C fan/425°F/Gas 7). Cut the fennel bulb into 1cm wedges; slice the green stalks into 2cm slices.

2. Spread the fennel wedges and chopped stalks in a single layer over the bottom of a large roasting pan. Drizzle with 1 tablespoon of the olive oil. Sprinkle with the allspice and 1 teaspoon of the cumin seeds. Season with salt and pepper to taste.

3. Roast the fennel mixture for 15 minutes or until the edges start to brown.

4. Stir in the tomatoes, butterbeans, and pomegranate molasses. Scatter the haloumi over the top. Drizzle with the remaining olive oil; sprinkle with the remaining cumin seeds. Roast for 25 minutes or until the haloumi is golden brown.

5. Scatter with the parsley leaves, and serve with the toasted pitta bread.

One-pan vegetable, olive, and herb filo pie

VEGETARIAN/ONE-PAN | PREP + COOK TIME **45 MINUTES** | SERVES **4**

PER SERVING | Energy kcals 634 | Carbohydrate 52g of which sugar 7g | Fat 36g of which saturates 9g | Salt 3.8g plus seasoning | Fibre 6g

Swiss chard is high in non-haem iron, which is important in a vegetarian diet. Iron from plant sources is not absorbed as well as haem iron from meat. Including vitamin C either in the dish (we used tomatoes in this recipe) or with the meal as a whole can aid absorption.

¼ cup (60ml) extra virgin olive oil

350g chestnut mushrooms, halved

2 tbsp lemon thyme leaves, finely chopped, plus extra 8 sprigs

4 garlic cloves, crushed

1 cup (180g) pitted Sicilian green olives

400g can diced tomatoes

500g Swiss chard, trimmed, coarsely chopped

⅓ cup (50g) pine nuts, toasted

150g haloumi, coarsely grated

6 sheets of filo pastry (thawed if frozen)

¼ cup (50g) couscous

salt and freshly ground black pepper

1 Preheat the oven to 220°C (200°C fan/425°F/Gas 7).

2 Heat 2 teaspoons of the olive oil in a deep 22cm (base measurement) ovenproof frying pan over a high heat. Cook the mushrooms, chopped lemon thyme, and garlic, stirring occasionally, for 5 minutes or until the mushrooms are golden. Season with salt and pepper to taste.

3 Coarsely chop three-quarters of the olives; leave the rest whole.

4 Add the tomatoes and chopped olives to the pan with the mushrooms; cook for 5 minutes or until thickened. Add the Swiss chard; cook, stirring, for 1 minute until wilted. Transfer to a large bowl; season with salt and pepper to taste. Set aside to cool. Wipe the pan clean and reserve. Finely chop ¼ cup (40g) of the pine nuts; combine with the haloumi in a small bowl.

5 Lightly brush the reserved pan with some of the remaining olive oil. Unwrap the filo and cover any sheets you aren't using immediately with baking parchment, then a damp tea towel. Lightly brush 1 sheet of filo with olive oil, and sprinkle with 2 tablespoons of the haloumi mixture. Top with a second sheet of filo. Repeat with the olive oil, haloumi mixture, and filo to create a stack of 3 sheets. Place in the frying pan, with the edges of the filo overhanging. Repeat with the remaining filo, olive oil, and haloumi mixture to create a second stack; place crossways in the frying pan. Sprinkle over the remaining haloumi mixture and the uncooked couscous.

6 Squeeze any excess liquid from the mushroom mixture. Spoon the cooled mushroom mixture into the pan. Fold over the filo to cover most of the pie, leaving a 6cm uncovered round in the centre for steam to escape. Brush the pastry top with the remaining oil. Set the pan on an oven tray.

7 Bake the pie for 18 minutes; top with the extra thyme sprigs and bake for a further 2 minutes or until golden. Serve topped with the remaining olives and pine nuts.

Broccoli and paneer saag curry

VEGETARIAN | PREP + COOK TIME **40 MINUTES** | SERVES **4**
PER SERVING | Energy kcals 567 | Carbohydrate 21g of which sugar 14g | Fat 32g of which saturates 17g | Salt 0.4g | Fibre 13g

Paneer is made by pressing cottage cheese curds to form blocks of cheese. It is rich in protein, with on average 100g of paneer providing 18.3g of protein. If you are dairy-intolerant, substitute the same weight of firm tofu for the paneer.

2 tbsp extra virgin olive oil

400g paneer, cut into 2cm pieces

800g broccoli, cut into florets

1 onion (150g), finely chopped

1 large bunch of coriander (150g), leaves reserved, stems and roots finely chopped

2 tbsp grated fresh root ginger

2 tsp garam masala

400g can diced tomatoes

2¹/₂ cups (625ml) vegetable stock

1 bunch of spinach (300g), washed, leaves picked

300g sugarsnap peas, trimmed

2 tbsp lemon juice

1 Heat 1 tablespoon of the olive oil in a large, deep frying pan over a high heat. Cook the paneer, turning, for 3 minutes or until golden on all sides. Transfer to a large bowl. Cook three-quarters of the broccoli for 3 minutes or until browned; add to the bowl with the paneer.

2 Reduce the heat to medium. Heat the remaining olive oil in the same pan; cook the onion, ¹/₂ cup (about 30g) of the coriander roots and stems, ginger, and garam masala for 5 minutes or until softened. Add the tomatoes and vegetable stock; bring to the boil. Cook for 8 minutes or until the stock has reduced slightly.

3 Process the remaining broccoli and spinach leaves until finely chopped. Stir into the curry.

4 Return the paneer and cooked broccoli to the pan, along with the sugarsnap peas; cook for 3 minutes or until warmed through. Stir through the lemon juice.

5 Serve the curry topped with the reserved coriander leaves.

TIP

Serve the curry with crisp wholemeal flatbreads or brown rice, if you like.

Tray-baked mussels, tomatoes, and butterbeans

HIGH-PROTEIN | PREP + COOK TIME **40 MINUTES** | SERVES **4**

PER SERVING | Energy kcals 454 | Carbohydrate 48g of which sugar 10g | Fat 9g of which saturates 1.5g | Salt 2.7g plus seasoning | Fibre 6g

A dozen mussels provide all the iron and vitamin B12 you need for the day, a third of your zinc, more than a third of your magnesium, and a tenth of your vitamin A. And all for very few calories and pretty much no saturated fat. Most of those calories come from protein, so opting for mussels can help to curb your appetite.

2 x 400g cans peeled cherry tomatoes

1/3 cup (65g) baby capers, drained

5 garlic cloves, thinly sliced

1 tsp smoked paprika

2 1/2 cups (175g) coarsely torn chunks of sourdough

1/2 tsp dried chilli flakes

1/4 cup (15g) finely chopped flat-leaf parsley leaves, plus extra sprigs, to serve

1 tbsp extra virgin olive oil

1.3kg pot-ready mussels

400g can butterbeans, drained, rinsed

2 1/2 cups (100g) firmly packed baby spinach leaves

salt and freshly ground black pepper

1 Preheat the oven to 220°C (200°C fan/425°F/Gas 7). Put the tomatoes, capers, 4 of the garlic cloves, and the paprika in a large, deep-sided heavy-based roasting pan. Cover with foil; cook for 20 minutes.

2 Meanwhile, put the breadcrumbs, chilli, parsley, and remaining garlic clove on a baking tray; drizzle over the oil. Season with salt and pepper to taste; toss well to combine. Set aside.

3 Discard any mussels with broken shells and remove any remaining beards.

4 Remove the foil from the roasting pan. Add the mussels and butterbeans; stir to combine. Cover again with the foil; cook for 15 minutes. Add the breadcrumbs to the oven; bake for 10 minutes or until golden, turning halfway during the cooking time.

5 Allow the mussels to stand, covered, for 5 minutes. Remove the foil, add the spinach, and toss to combine. Serve the tray bake topped with the toasted breadcrumbs and the extra parsley sprigs.

Courgette koftas with smoky tomato aïoli

VEGETARIAN | PREP + COOK TIME **45 MINUTES** | SERVES **4**

PER SERVING | Energy kcals 505 | Carbohydrate 33g of which sugar 4.5g | Fat 38g of which saturates 3.5g | Salt 0.3g plus seasoning | Fibre 4g

For a relaxed lunch or picnic, serve the koftas stuffed into wholegrain pitta bread with a
bitter green salad dressed with lemon juice, or pair with one of the other vegetarian recipes
in this chapter as part of a mezze spread.

250g all-purpose potatoes, scrubbed, halved

500g courgettes, coarsely grated

1 long green chilli, finely chopped

4 spring onions, finely chopped

1/2 cup (90g) rice flour

sunflower oil for shallow-frying

salt and freshly ground black pepper

micro sorrel or other soft-leaf herb, to serve

smoky tomato aïoli

2 tbsp chopped sun-dried tomatoes

1 chipotle chilli in adobo sauce

1 garlic clove, chopped

1/2 cup (150g) whole-egg mayonnaise

1 Put the potatoes in a small saucepan; cover with water. Bring to the boil; cook for 25 minutes or until tender. Drain, return to the pan, and coarsely mash with a fork.

2 Meanwhile, to make the smoky tomato aïoli, put the sun-dried tomatoes in a small bowl; cover with boiling water. Allow to stand for 15 minutes; drain. Stir through the remaining aïoli ingredients until combined (or blend until smooth); season with salt and pepper to taste.

3 Place the grated courgettes in a clean tea towel; twist the ends together, and squeeze over the sink to remove any excess moisture. Put the courgette in a large bowl; add the mashed potato, chilli, spring onions, and rice flour. Season with salt and pepper to taste; mix well to combine.

4 Heat enough sunflower oil to reach a depth of 2cm in a large frying pan over a high heat. Shape 1/4-cup measures of the courgette mixture into ovals to make 12 koftas in total. Shallow-fry, in batches, for 3 minutes on each side or until golden and crisp. Remove with a slotted spoon; drain on kitchen paper.

5 Scatter the koftas with the micro sorrel; serve with the aïoli.

TIP

You can substitute 1/2 teaspoon smoked paprika
and a pinch of chilli powder for the chipotle chilli
in adobo sauce used in the aïoli.

Indian-roasted chilli, tomato, and chickpeas

VEGETARIAN | PREP + COOK TIME **30 MINUTES** | SERVES **4 AS PART OF A FEAST**

PER SERVING | Energy kcals 387 | Carbohydrate 22g of which sugar 6g | Fat 27g of which saturates 5g | Salt 0.8g plus seasoning | Fibre 6.5g

As well as being rich in plant protein, chickpeas pack a pretty powerful nutritional punch
for such unassuming-looking seeds. They provide slow-release, low-GI carbohydrates,
stacks of fibre, essential minerals, and beneficial plant chemicals.

400g can chickpeas, drained, rinsed

6 long red chillies

1^1/$_2$ tsp brown mustard seeds

2 tsp cumin seeds

^{1}/$_2$ tsp dried chilli flakes

2 tsp ground turmeric

^{1}/$_3$ cup (80ml) extra virgin olive oil

2 tbsp curry leaves, plus extra 3 sprigs

500g ripe cherry vine tomatoes, cut into
small clusters

8 poppadoms

^{1}/$_2$ cup (140g) Greek-style yogurt

salt and freshly ground black pepper

1 Preheat the oven to 200°C (180°C fan/400°F/Gas 6). Line a large baking
tray with baking parchment.

2 Line another large tray with a clean tea towel. Spread the chickpeas on
the towel to absorb any excess moisture.

3 Cut the chillies in half lengthways, keeping the stalk attached; remove
and discard the seeds. Combine the mustard and cumin seeds, chilli
flakes, turmeric, olive oil, and curry leaves in a large bowl. Add the
chillies, chickpeas, and tomatoes. Season with salt and pepper to taste;
toss gently to combine.

4 Spread out the mixture over the prepared tray. Top with the extra sprigs
of curry leaves. Bake, turning occasionally, for 15 minutes or until the
tomatoes collapse and the chillies are tender.

5 Meanwhile, cook the poppadoms according to the packet directions.

6 Swirl a little of the tomato cooking juices through the yogurt.
Serve the chickpea mixture with the yogurt sauce and poppadoms.

Golden cauliflower paella

HIGH-PROTEIN | PREP + COOK TIME **45 MINUTES** | SERVES **6**
PER SERVING | Energy kcals 314 | Carbohydrate 22g of which sugar 12g | Fat 8g of which saturates 1.5g | Salt 2.2g plus seasoning | Fibre 9g

Cauliflower replaces white rice in this dish for a lower carbohydrate version of paella.
A seafood marinara mix that includes fish, prawns, and octopus will provide good levels of
the long-chain omega-3 fats that are anti-inflammatory and therefore can be helpful in
relieving all sorts of inflammatory conditions.

1 cauliflower (1.5kg), cut into florets

2 small red peppers (300g)

2 tbsp extra virgin olive oil

8 shallots (200g), halved

1 tsp ground turmeric

1 tsp smoked paprika

2 cups (500ml) chicken stock

400g can chickpeas, drained, rinsed

300g shelled uncooked prawns, tails intact

200g uncooked calamari rings

100g uncooked octopus pieces

200g skinless firm white fish fillets, cut into chunks

260g Sweet Berry baby vine tomatoes or cherry vine tomatoes

1/3 cup (15g) finely chopped flat-leaf parsley

salt and freshly ground black pepper

1 lemon (140g), cut into cheeks, to serve

chargrilled bread, to serve (optional)

1 Process the cauliflower, in batches, until it reaches the consistency of coarse breadcrumbs. Thinly slice 1 of the red peppers; chop the remaining pepper into 1cm pieces.

2 Heat the olive oil in a 34cm (1 litre/4-cup) round paella pan over a medium-high heat. Cook the shallots and chopped red pepper, stirring occasionally, for 5 minutes or until starting to brown and soften.

3 Add the cauliflower, turmeric, and smoked paprika; season with salt and pepper to taste. Cook, stirring continuously, for 2 minutes or until the cauliflower is heated through. Add the chicken stock, chickpeas, and sliced red pepper; cook, without stirring, for 10 minutes.

4 Add the seafood, fish, and tomatoes to the surface of the cauliflower mixture, pushing any large pieces of seafood into the mixture to submerge slightly. Cook for 5 minutes or until the liquid has been absorbed and the seafood is cooked through. Remove from the heat; allow the paella to stand for 5 minutes.

5 Scatter the paella with the parsley. Serve straight from the pan with the lemon cheeks for squeezing over and chargrilled bread for mopping up juices, if you like.

TIP

It is best to cook a paella over 2 burners so that heat is evenly distributed.

Pork with fennel and apple hash browns

HIGH-PROTEIN | PREP + COOK TIME **40 MINUTES** | SERVES **4**

PER SERVING | Energy kcals 541 | Carbohydrate 44g of which sugar 23g | Fat 21g of which saturates 4g | Salt 0.6g plus seasoning | Fibre 10g

Pork is strictly speaking a red meat; however, nutritionally its profile is closer to white meat. Although it is perceived as being a fatty meat, pork breeding has changed in recent years and in fact most pork today is pretty lean. It is also rich in thiamine, which plays an essential role in metabolism.

$\frac{1}{3}$ cup (80ml) extra virgin olive oil

2 tbsp apple cider vinegar

2 tbsp wholegrain mustard

2 tbsp runny honey

600g pork fillet, trimmed

2 fennel bulbs (600g), trimmed, fronds reserved

1 large all-purpose potato, scrubbed (300g)

2 large red eating apples (400g), halved, core removed

$\frac{1}{4}$ cup (40g) wholemeal plain flour

$\frac{1}{4}$ small red cabbage (200g), finely shaved

salt and freshly ground black pepper

1 Put 2 tablespoons of the olive oil, the vinegar, wholegrain mustard, and honey in a jug; stir until well combined. Put $\frac{1}{4}$ cup (60ml) of the dressing and the pork in a bowl. Season with salt and pepper to taste; toss to coat the pork evenly with the dressing.

2 To make the hash browns, coarsely grate the fennel, potato, and 1 of the apples. Combine the grated mixture in a clean tea towel; twist the ends of the towel and squeeze firmly over a sink to remove any excess liquid. Transfer the mixture to a large bowl, stir through the flour and 1 tablespoon chopped fennel fronds; season with salt and pepper to taste. Shape the mixture into 4 flat patty shapes.

3 Heat the remaining olive oil in a large non-stick frying pan over a medium-high heat. Cook the hash browns for 4 minutes on each side or until golden brown.

4 Meanwhile, preheat a medium non-stick frying pan to a high heat. Cook the pork for 4 minutes on each side or until browned and cooked as desired. Allow the pork to rest, covered, in the pan for 2 minutes. Transfer any pan juices to a small jug to serve.

5 Slice the remaining apple thinly; toss with the cabbage and remaining dressing. Serve the sliced pork and hash browns with the salad and any pan juices, topped with the remaining fennel fronds.

Braised balsamic lentils and butternut squash

VEGETARIAN | PREP + COOK TIME **1 HOUR 25 MINUTES** | SERVES **4**

PER SERVING | Energy kcals 411 | Carbohydrate 47g of which sugar 26g | Fat 15g of which saturates 6g | Salt 0.6g plus seasoning | Fibre 14g

Pulses contain phytates, which have received some bad press mostly on account of their ability to bind minerals such as iron, lowering absorption; overall phytates have been associated with beneficial effects. By consuming a varied diet with plenty of foods rich in minerals, you need not be concerned.

1.5kg whole butternut squash, skin washed

2 tbsp extra virgin olive oil

2 large carrots (360g), cut into 4 pieces

4 shallots (100g), peeled

8 sprigs of thyme

6 garlic cloves, unpeeled

1 cup (250ml) vegetable stock

400g can brown lentils, drained, rinsed

$\frac{1}{4}$ cup (60ml) caramelized balsamic vinegar

120g goat's curd, crumbled

salt and freshly ground black pepper

1 Preheat the oven to 200°C (180°C fan/400°F/Gas 6).

2 Cut the butternut squash in half lengthways, cutting from the base through to the stalk end. (Take care, as the stalk end is particularly hard.) Using a metal spoon, remove and discard the seeds. Make 4 cuts widthways, three-quarters of the way down into the flesh of each squash half, without reaching the skin.

3 Place the squash halves, cut-side up, in a deep roasting pan. Season generously with salt and pepper; drizzle with the olive oil. Add the carrots, shallots, 6 of the thyme sprigs, and garlic to the pan. Pour over the vegetable stock combined with $\frac{1}{2}$ cup (125ml) water. Cover the pan tightly with 2 layers of foil.

4 Bake the butternut squash for 45 minutes until just tender (depending on the thickness of the squash, it may require an additional 10 minutes). Remove the pan from the oven. Uncover carefully and scatter over the lentils. Drizzle with the balsamic vinegar.

5 Increase the oven temperature to 220°C (200°C fan/425°F/Gas 7). Roast the squash and lentils, uncovered, for a further 15 minutes or until the squash flesh is starting to brown and the braising liquid has reduced in volume by half.

6 Serve the roasted vegetables and lentils topped with the goat's curd and remaining 2 sprigs of thyme.

TIP

Make sure the roasting pan is just large enough to fit the ingredients. If it is too large, the liquid will evaporate too quickly.

Swiss chard dolmades

VEGETARIAN | PREP + COOK TIME **55 MINUTES** | SERVES **4**

PER SERVING | Energy kcals 682 | Carbohydrate 70g of which sugar 19g | Fat 31g of which saturates 13g | Salt 3.3g plus seasoning | Fibre 9g

Two of the world's healthiest diets, the Mediterranean and the Okinawan, have a few common features – one of those is their inclusion of dark leafy greens. Leafy greens are fabulous foods to eat every day. Low in calories and carbs, they have almost no effect on blood glucose.

500g microwave or instant brown rice

200g fresh firm ricotta

2 tsp finely grated lemon zest

1/2 tsp ground cinnamon

2 tbsp chopped fresh dill, plus extra sprigs, to serve

2 tbsp currants

200g soft feta, crumbled

8 large Swiss chard leaves (480g), stems removed

2 x 400g jars arrabbiata pasta sauce

200g wholegrain sourdough bread, coarsely chopped

2 tbsp extra virgin olive oil

salt and freshly ground black pepper

1   Preheat the oven to 200°C (180°C fan/400°F/Gas 6).

2   Heat the rice according to the packet directions; put in a large bowl with the ricotta, lemon zest, cinnamon, 2 tablespoons chopped dill, currants, and half of the feta. Season with salt and pepper to taste.

3   Place the chard leaves side by side on a clean work surface. Divide the rice mixture evenly among the chard leaves, placing it at one end of each leaf. Roll up the leaves tightly, folding in the sides as you roll. Arrange the dolmades side by side in a 21cm x 32cm ovenproof dish. Pour over the arrabbiata pasta sauce.

4   Process the sourdough bread until coarse crumbs form. Toss the crumbs with the olive oil to combine; scatter over the top of the dolmades with the remaining feta. Bake for 30 minutes, covering halfway through the cooking time if the feta is browning too quickly, or until the crumbs and feta are golden. Serve topped with the extra dill sprigs.

TIPS

- Instead of a spicy pasta sauce, you can use a mild variety if you like.
- Make sure that you select 8 large Swiss chard leaves that are equal in size for even cooking.

Lentil and vegetable stuffed tomatoes

VEGETARIAN | PREP + COOK TIME **40 MINUTES** | SERVES **4**

PER SERVING | Energy kcals 402 | Carbohydrate 22g of which sugar 15g | Fat 25g of which saturates 9g | Salt 1.3g plus seasoning | Fibre 10g

The three standout ingredients in this recipe are lentils, tomatoes, and walnuts. Both the lentils and walnuts contribute fibre and protein. Walnuts are an impressive source of plant omega-3 fat alpha–linolenic acid (ALA), with 30g walnuts providing 1.9g. ALA cannot be made in the body and must be obtained from our diet. It seems to play a role in heart health.

8 large vine-ripened tomatoes (1.75kg)

1 fennel bulb (300g), trimmed, fronds reserved

400g can brown lentils, drained, rinsed

2 garlic cloves, crushed

$1/4$ cup (10g) finely chopped fresh dill

1 tsp ground cumin

1 tsp dried mint

$1/2$ cup (50g) coarsely chopped roasted walnuts

200g firm feta, cut into 3cm pieces

2 tbsp extra virgin olive oil

1 tsp finely grated lemon zest

salt and freshly ground black pepper

1 Preheat the oven to 220°C (200°C fan/425°F/Gas 7). Line a baking tray with baking parchment.

2 Slice the tops off the tomatoes; reserve. Using a small spoon, scoop out the flesh from each tomato; reserve $1/4$ cup tomato pulp. Place the tomatoes on the prepared tray.

3 Trim $1/3$ cup fronds from the fennel bulb; reserve. Chop the remaining fronds. Slice the fennel stalks into rounds; cut the bulb into wedges. Combine the lentils, garlic, dill, chopped fennel fronds, cumin, mint, walnuts, and reserved tomato pulp in a bowl. Mix well; season with salt and pepper to taste.

4 Spoon the lentil mixture into each tomato cavity, pressing down firmly; cover with the reserved tomato tops. Place the fennel slices and wedges with the feta on the tray between the tomatoes. Drizzle with half of the olive oil. Season with salt and pepper to taste. Cook for 15 minutes or until the tomatoes are tender.

5 Remove the tomatoes from the oven; cover to keep warm. Continue to cook the fennel and feta for a further 15 minutes or until golden brown. Return the tomatoes to the tray; scatter with the lemon zest and the reserved fennel fronds. Drizzle with the remaining olive oil.

Mexican chicken tray bake

HIGH-PROTEIN | PREP + COOK TIME **1 HOUR 5 MINUTES** | SERVES **4**
PER SERVING | Energy kcals 490 | Carbohydrate 41g of which sugar 13g | Fat 12g of which saturates 3g | Salt 0.8g plus seasoning | Fibre 11g

Using skinless chicken legs helps to reduce the fat content of this dish. It also allows
the chicken meat to absorb the smoky herbs and spices more readily, upping the intensity
of the flavours. Serve with light soured cream, if you like.

750g skinless French-boned chicken legs, trimmed (see tip)

2 tsp smoked paprika

2 tsp ground coriander

1 tbsp extra virgin olive oil

400g arrabbiata pasta sauce

2 cups (500ml) chicken stock

½ cup (100g) brown basmati rice

400g can red kidney beans, drained, rinsed

2 red peppers (400g), quartered, stems left intact

1 red onion (170g), cut into thin wedges

salt and freshly ground black pepper

1 cup (30g) coriander leaves, to serve

lime wedges, to serve

1 Preheat the oven to 180°C (160°C fan/350°F/Gas 4).

2 Coat the chicken in the combined smoked paprika and ground coriander. Heat the oil in a large flameproof roasting pan or casserole dish. Brown the chicken for 3 minutes on each side or until lightly golden.

3 Add the pasta sauce, stock, rice, kidney beans, red peppers, and onion to the pan. Season with salt and pepper to taste; bring to a simmer.

4 Transfer to the oven; bake, covered, for 30 minutes. Remove the lid; cook, uncovered, for a further 10 minutes or until the chicken is cooked through and the rice is tender. Allow to stand for 5 minutes; serve topped with the coriander leaves and with lime wedges for squeezing over.

TIP

French boning is an aesthetic technique where the end of the bone is trimmed and the bone scraped clean; racks of lamb are one example. If your poultry supplier doesn't have French-boned chicken legs, use 8 chicken legs, with the skin removed, instead.

Sticky cumin lamb with beetroot and feta salad

HIGH-PROTEIN | PREP + COOK TIME **30 MINUTES** | SERVES **6**

PER SERVING | Energy kcals 508 | Carbohydrate 20g of which sugar 14g | Fat 30g of which saturates 11g | Salt 1.3g plus seasoning | Fibre 5.5g

Red meat is a fabulous source of high-quality protein. Research has pretty conclusively shown that high-protein diets help us to control our weight and most importantly keep off any lost weight. Always choose good-quality red meat and be judicious in how much you eat.

800g lamb leg steaks

¼ cup (60ml) extra virgin olive oil

1 tbsp runny honey

2 tsp cumin seeds, toasted

500g cooked baby beetroot (see tip)

400g can brown lentils, drained, rinsed

¼ cup (60ml) balsamic vinegar

120g red cabbage, thinly sliced

200g firm feta

8 spring onions

⅓ cup (35g) coarsely chopped walnuts, roasted

salt and freshly ground black pepper

1 Preheat a ridged cast-iron grill pan or frying pan to a high heat.

2 Combine the lamb, 1 tablespoon of the olive oil, honey, and cumin in a bowl; season. Allow to stand for 15 minutes.

3 Put the beetroot, lentils, vinegar, and remaining olive oil in a bowl; season with salt and pepper to taste. Toss well to coat. Arrange the cabbage on a platter with the beetroot and lentil mixture.

4 Pat the feta dry between layers of kitchen paper. Place a piece of baking parchment in the grill pan; top with the feta. Cook for 3 minutes or until grill marks appear and the feta starts to brown around the edges. Top with another piece of baking parchment. Using a wide spatula, turn the feta over; cook for a further 3 minutes or until charred. Remove from the pan; carefully peel off the paper and place the feta on the salad.

5 Meanwhile, chargrill the lamb for 3 minutes on each side or until cooked to your liking. Transfer to a plate; allow the lamb to rest, loosely covered with foil. Chargrill the spring onions for 2 minutes on each side or until just softened and charred. Slice the lamb; serve with the salad, spring onions, and chopped walnuts.

TIP

To roast 1 bunch of fresh baby beetroot, trim the stems and scrub. Wrap the beetroot in foil. Roast at 200°C (180°C fan/400°F/Gas 6) for 40 minutes or until tender; cool, then peel.

Ginger-roasted sea trout with pickled beetroot and couscous

FAST | PREP + COOK TIME **25 MINUTES** | SERVES **4**

PER SERVING | Energy kcals 436 | Carbohydrate 26g of which sugar 15g | Fat 15g of which saturates 1g | Salt 0.7g plus seasoning | Fibre 6g

The punchy flavours in this citrussy marinade work well with other oily fish such as salmon, mackerel, or sardines. Sea, or ocean, trout is used here, but you could replace with salmon fillets, if you like. Keep the skin on for cooking; you can always peel it away afterwards.

2 small beetroots (200g)

2 tbsp white balsamic vinegar

pinch of salt

2 oranges (480g)

1 tbsp grated fresh root ginger

2 tsp cumin seeds

2 tbsp extra virgin olive oil

4 x 200g sea trout fillets, skin on

³/₄ cup (150g) wholewheat couscous

¹/₃ cup (10g) coarsely chopped flat-leaf parsley

350g watercress, trimmed

salt and freshly ground black pepper

1 Preheat the oven to 180°C (160°C fan/350°F/Gas 4). Line a baking tray with baking parchment.

2 Peel the beetroots. Using a mandolin, V-slicer, or wide vegetable peeler, shave the beetroot into rounds. Place in a bowl with the balsamic vinegar and a pinch of salt; set aside until needed.

3 To make the marinade, finely grate 2 teaspoons of zest from one of the oranges into a small bowl. Squeeze the juice from 1 orange. Add 2 tablespoons to the same bowl; reserve the remaining juice. Next, add the ginger, cumin, and 1 tablespoon of the olive oil; season with salt and pepper to taste. Cut the zest and white pith from the remaining orange, then use a sharp knife to cut the flesh into rounds. Halve the rounds; set aside to serve.

4 Score 2 slashes about 2cm deep lengthways into the skin side of the fish fillets. Rub half of the marinade all over the fish and into the scored slits; place on the prepared tray and spoon over the remaining marinade. Bake the fish for 10 minutes or until just cooked through.

5 Meanwhile, put the couscous in a large heatproof bowl; pour over ³/₄ cup (180ml) boiling water and cover. Allow to stand for 5 minutes; fluff up the grains with a fork. Toss through the parsley and 2 tablespoons of the reserved orange juice; season with salt and pepper to taste.

6 Spoon the couscous onto a platter; add the watercress, drained pickled beetroot, and orange slices. Drizzle with the remaining olive oil. Top with the trout fillets, drizzling over any pan juices, and serve.

SWEET

Indulging a sweet tooth need not mean
abandoning healthier eating for culinary sin.
Special indulgences, fruit-filled goodness,
treats for elevenses – all are found here.

Beetroot red velvet waffles

GLUTEN-FREE | PREP + COOK TIME **45 MINUTES** | MAKES **8**

PER SERVING | Energy kcals 289 | Carbohydrate 27g of which sugar 19g | Fat 15g of which saturates 2g | Salt 0.5g | Fibre 3g

The berries in the compote are high in vitamin C and contain many potentially beneficial plant chemicals that have been shown to have anti-viral and anti-bacterial properties, while the waffles contain beetroot, which is a great source of fibre, minerals, and vitamin C.

1/4 cup (25g) cocoa powder

1/2 cup (60g) cornflour

1 1/2 cups (180g) almond meal

1 tsp bicarbonate of soda

1 large beetroot (200g), finely grated

1 cup (250ml) buttermilk

1 tsp vanilla bean paste

2 tbsp runny honey

2 eggs, separated

olive oil cooking spray for greasing

sifted icing sugar, to dust (optional)

berry compote

1/4 cup (90g) runny honey

2 tsp vanilla bean paste

500g frozen mixed berries, thawed

1   Sift the cocoa, cornflour, almond meal, and bicarbonate of soda into a large bowl, pushing the mixture through with a spatula. Add the grated beetroot, buttermilk, vanilla, honey, and egg yolks; mix to combine.

2   Whisk the egg whites and a pinch of salt using an electric mixer until stiff peaks form. Gently fold the whites into the beetroot mixture; allow to stand for 10 minutes.

3   Meanwhile, to make the berry compote, heat the honey and vanilla in a large frying pan over a high heat until boiling. Add the berries; cook, stirring, for 4 minutes or until the juices are released.

4   Lightly grease a waffle iron with cooking spray; heat according to the manufacturer's instructions. Working in batches, add 1/3 cup batter to the iron; cook for 3 minutes or until cooked through. Remove and set aside to keep warm. Repeat with the remaining batter to make 8 waffles in total.

5   Serve the waffles topped with the berry compote and dusted with a little icing sugar, if you like.

TIP

You can customize the compote using other seasonal fruit. Try the same weight of figs and a handful of grapes, and swap out the almond meal for hazelnut meal instead.

Banoffee mousse pots

FAST | PREP + COOK TIME **15 MINUTES + FREEZING** | SERVES **6**
PER SERVING | Energy kcals 688 | Carbohydrate 77g of which sugar 62g | Fat 37g of which saturates 26g | Salt 0.4g | Fibre 5g

Traditionally banoffee pie is a sugar-laden treat. We've reworked the original using coconut cream in place of cream and the natural sweetness of dates in place of sweetened condensed milk. It is still a special-occasion-only treat, though, because of its fat content.

2 x 400ml cans pure coconut cream, refrigerated (see tip)

6 large bananas (1.38kg)

1 tbsp runny honey, plus extra, to serve (optional)

1 tsp vanilla bean paste

1 cup (230g) firmly packed pitted fresh dates

$1/4$ cup (70g) smooth natural peanut butter

$1/2$ tsp ground cinnamon

$1/4$ tsp sea salt flakes

50g dark chocolate (70% cocoa), coarsely chopped

1 Scoop the thick cream from the top of the cans of coconut cream. You will need 2 cups (500ml) cream. Reserve the remaining liquid.

2 Peel 5 of the bananas; process with the thick coconut cream, honey, and vanilla until completely smooth. Divide evenly among six 1-cup (250ml) glasses. Place on a tray and freeze for 1 hour.

3 Meanwhile, process $3/4$ cup (180ml) of the reserved coconut liquid with the dates, peanut butter, cinnamon, and salt until completely smooth. Divide the mixture evenly over the tops of the semi-set mousse pots. Return to the freezer for 1 hour or until slightly firm.

4 Peel the remaining banana; cut on a diagonal into small pieces. Top the mousse pots with the banana and the chopped chocolate. Drizzle with extra honey, if you like.

TIPS

- You will need to buy coconut cream without emulsifiers, so that the thick cream sits on top of the liquid.
- If you freeze the mousse pots for longer than 1 hour, thaw at room temperature for 25 minutes before serving.

Blueberry and ricotta hand pies

DO-AHEAD/PORTABLE | PREP + COOK TIME **55 MINUTES** | MAKES **6**
PER SERVING | Energy kcals 355 | Carbohydrate 35g of which sugar 15g | Fat 19g of which saturates 4g | Salt 0.1g | Fibre 3g

Oozing with creaminess laced with concentrated bursts of berry goodness, these hand pies
are not as sinful a treat as you might think. For a touch more of a flavour hit, serve them
dusted with icing sugar and topped with extra strips of lemon zest, if you like.

1 cup (160g) plain wholemeal flour

$1/3$ cup (40g) ground almonds

$1/3$ cup (50g) coconut sugar, plus extra 2 tsp
for sprinkling

200g fresh soft ricotta

$1/4$ cup (60ml) extra virgin olive oil

2 tbsp ice-cold water

250g blueberries

1 tbsp finely grated lemon zest

2 tbsp lemon juice

1 tbsp cornflour

1 egg, lightly beaten

1 Preheat the oven to 180°C (160°C fan/350°F/Gas 4). Line a baking tray with
baking parchment.

2 Process the flour, ground almonds, and 2 teaspoons of the $1/3$ cup (50g)
coconut sugar until combined. Add the ricotta, olive oil, and
2 tablespoons ice-cold water; pulse until the dough starts to come
together. Transfer to a work surface and gently knead to bring the dough
together. Cut the dough in half, shape each half into a disc, and enclose
in cling film. Leave to chill in the fridge for 30 minutes.

3 Meanwhile, put the blueberries, remaining coconut sugar, lemon zest
and juice, and cornflour in a medium saucepan. Cook, stirring and lightly
crushing some of the berries, over a medium heat for 4 minutes or until
the mixture thickens. Transfer to a bowl; cool slightly.

4 Roll out half of the dough on a lightly floured surface to 2mm thick.
Using a 9cm cutter, cut out six rounds. Place on the prepared tray.
Divide the berry filling evenly among the rounds, leaving a 1cm border
around the edges. Lightly brush the edges of the dough with the beaten
egg. Roll out the remaining dough on a lightly floured surface; cut out six
10.5cm rounds. Cover the pies with the larger rounds, pressing down on
the edges with a fork to seal. Lightly brush the tops with more of the
beaten egg and sprinkle with the extra coconut sugar. Using a sharp
knife, cut two 2cm slashes in the top of each pie.

5 Bake for 25 minutes or until golden brown. Serve the hand pies warm
or cold.

TIP

You can also make the hand pies using raspberries
instead of blueberries, or use ground hazelnuts in
place of the ground almonds.

15-minute strawberry and coconut sticky rice pudding

FAST | PREP + COOK TIME **15 MINUTES** | SERVES **4**

PER SERVING | Energy kcals 695 | Carbohydrate 71g of which sugar 25g | Fat 38g of which saturates 20g | Salt 0.6g | Fibre 8g

Mango with sticky rice is a traditional and extremely popular sweet treat in Thailand and other parts of Southeast Asia such as Laos and Vietnam. Here, it is given a less traditional treatment with brown rice in place of the usual glutinous rice. It's not an everyday treat because of the coconut cream, so save it for a special occasion.

500g microwave or instant brown rice

400ml can coconut cream

¾ cup (60g) quinoa flakes

¼ cup (70g) cashew spread

¼ cup (60ml) pure maple syrup, plus extra 2 tbsp, to serve (see tips)

1 tsp ground cinnamon

pinch of sea salt flakes

1 lime (90g)

400g strawberries

¼ cup (35g) pistachios, coarsely chopped

1 Combine the rice, coconut cream, quinoa, cashew spread, half of the maple syrup, cinnamon, sea salt flakes, and 2 cups (500ml) water in a large, heavy-based saucepan over a medium-high heat. Cook, stirring continuously, for 10 minutes or until the mixture is soft and creamy in texture.

2 Meanwhile, finely grate the zest from the lime (you will need 1 teaspoon of zest). Reserve. Squeeze the juice from the lime (you will need 1 tablespoon of juice). Put 300g of the strawberries in a small saucepan with the remaining maple syrup and the lime juice. Cook, stirring, over a medium-high heat for 10 minutes or until thickened slightly and the strawberries have broken down.

3 Top the hot rice pudding with the warm strawberry compote, remaining strawberries, pistachios, reserved lime zest, and the extra 2 tablespoons maple syrup to taste. Serve immediately.

TIPS

- Add the maple syrup to taste, depending on the sweetness of the strawberries.
- The pudding thickens on standing, so stir in a little extra water to loosen if reheating.

Chocolate mousse with blackberries and hazelnut crunch

FAST | PREP + COOK TIME **20 MINUTES + REFRIGERATION** | SERVES **4**

PER SERVING | Energy kcals 442 | Carbohydrate 31g of which sugar 28g | Fat 27g of which saturates 9g | Salt 0.3g | Fibre 6g

Chocolate does more than simply taste good and lift your mood. But to get the health benefits look to pure cocoa and dark chocolate with at least 70% cocoa solids. Not only is it packed with minerals and antioxidants, but it may help to lower blood pressure and cholesterol too.

$^1/_2$ cup (70g) hazelnuts

$^1/_4$ cup (60ml) pure maple syrup

$^1/_4$ cup (25g) coconut milk powder

$^1/_2$ tsp sea salt flakes

1$^1/_2$ cups (225g) frozen blackberries

100g dark chocolate (85% cocoa), chopped

300g silken tofu, drained

1   Preheat the oven to 180°C (160°C fan/350°F/Gas 4). Line a baking tray with baking parchment.

2   Toss the hazelnuts with 2 teaspoons of the maple syrup, 2 teaspoons of the coconut milk powder, and the sea salt on the prepared tray. Bake for 8 minutes or until dark golden and caramelized. Allow to cool on the tray, then coarsely chop the resulting hazelnut crunch.

3   Meanwhile, put the blackberries in a small saucepan with 1 tablespoon of the maple syrup and 1 tablespoon water. Bring to a simmer; cook for 5 minutes or until the berries start to break down and release their juices. Refrigerate for 10 minutes.

4   Put the chocolate in a glass heatproof bowl. Microwave on HIGH (100%) in 30-second bursts, stirring between each one, until the chocolate is melted and smooth. Allow to cool for 5 minutes.

5   Process the melted chocolate, tofu, remaining coconut milk powder, and remaining maple syrup until very smooth.

6   Spoon three-quarters of the berry mixture into four 1-cup (250ml) serving dishes or glasses. Top with the chocolate mousse mixture. Refrigerate for 4 hours or overnight. Spoon over the remaining berry mixture. Serve sprinkled with the hazelnut crunch.

Gluten-free pancakes with strawberries

GLUTEN-FREE | PREP + COOK TIME **45 MINUTES** | MAKES **8**

PER SERVING | Energy kcals 252 | Carbohydrate 26g of which sugar 12g | Fat 12g of which saturates 3g | Salt 0.7g | Fibre 3g

Quinoa flour and almond meal replace refined white flour in the pancake recipe here to make a more wholesome option that will suit coeliacs. To make the recipe dairy-free, too, swap the Greek-style yogurt for your favourite non-dairy variety.

200g quinoa flour

3 tsp gluten-free baking powder

$^2/_3$ cup (80g) almond meal

2 cups (500ml) almond milk

$^1/_3$ cup (80ml) pure maple syrup, plus extra 1 tbsp, to serve

2 eggs, lightly beaten

extra virgin olive oil cooking spray

$^2/_3$ cup (190g) Greek-style yogurt

250g strawberries, halved

1 Sift the quinoa flour and baking powder into a large bowl; stir in the almond meal.

2 Combine the almond milk, $^1/_3$ cup (80ml) maple syrup, and beaten eggs in a jug. Stir into the dry ingredients until well combined.

3 Spray a small 20cm (14cm base measurement) non-stick frying pan with olive oil, then heat over a medium heat. Pour in $^1/_2$ cup of the batter; cook for 3 minutes or until bubbles appear on the surface. Turn; cook for a further 1 minute or until golden underneath. Remove from the pan; cover to keep warm. Repeat to make 8 pancakes in total.

4 Top the pancakes with the yogurt and strawberries. Drizzle with the extra 1 tablespoon maple syrup, and serve.

Peach and yogurt tiramisu pots

FAST | PREP + COOK TIME **15 MINUTES** | SERVES **4**

PER SERVING | Energy kcals 553 | Carbohydrate 57g of which sugar 49g | Fat 27g of which saturates 14g | Salt 0.4g | Fibre 5g

This healthier makeover of the classic tiramisu ditches mascarpone in favour of a mixture of lower-fat ricotta and Greek-style yogurt, while the addition of peaches will contribute towards your daily fruit and vegetable intake.

300g fresh ricotta

1$\frac{1}{3}$ cups (375g) Greek-style yogurt

2$\frac{1}{2}$ tbsp runny honey

1 large orange (300g)

8 sponge finger biscuits (95g)

40g dark chocolate (70% cocoa), finely grated

4 yellow peaches (600g), halved, cut into thin wedges

2 tbsp pine nuts

1 Process the ricotta, $\frac{1}{3}$ cup (80ml) of the yogurt, and 1 tablespoon of the honey until smooth. Transfer to a bowl; fold in the remaining yogurt. Refrigerate until needed.

2 Using a zesting tool, remove the zest from the orange in long strips; reserve to serve (alternatively, you can finely grate the zest). Juice the orange; you will need $\frac{1}{3}$ cup (80ml) of juice. Put the orange juice and 2 teaspoons of the honey in a bowl; whisk to combine.

3 Break the biscuits into thirds. Place 3 pieces into the bottom of each of four 1-cup (250ml) glasses; drizzle with half of the orange mixture. Top with half of the ricotta mixture. Sprinkle with half of the grated chocolate and peach wedges. Repeat the layers with the remaining biscuit thirds, orange mixture, ricotta mixture, grated chocolate, and peach wedges.

4 Toss the pine nuts in the remaining 1$\frac{1}{2}$ tablespoons honey. Microwave on HIGH (100%) for 50 seconds or until the honey and pine nuts are golden.

5 Divide the hot caramelized pine nuts among the tiramisu pots. Serve scattered with the reserved orange zest.

TIP

Use a Microplane grater, if you have one, to grate the chocolate very finely.

Wholemeal-crust chocolate fudge pie

DAIRY-FREE | PREP + COOK TIME **1 HOUR 30 MINUTES** | SERVES **10**

PER SERVING | Energy kcals 485 | Carbohydrate 58g of which sugar 28g | Fat 23g of which saturates 15g | Salt 0.3g | Fibre 6g

This clever pie utilizes the natural sweetness of orange sweet potato and honey in place of refined sugars. The sweet potato also adds fibre, a good array of B vitamins and vitamin C, while hazelnuts provide predominantly monounsaturated fats.

1kg small orange sweet potatoes, halved

2 eggs

200g dark chocolate (70% cocoa), melted, cooled

1/4 cup (90g) runny honey

2 tbsp wholemeal plain flour

1 cup (250ml) canned coconut milk

2 tsp vanilla bean paste

1 tsp Dutch-process cocoa powder (see tip)

1 cup (280g) dairy-free coconut yogurt, to serve

wholemeal pie crust

1/3 cup (35g) hazelnut meal

1/3 cup (30g) rolled oats

1 cup (160g) wholemeal plain flour

1/4 cup (55g) coconut oil

pinch of salt

1/3 cup (80ml) ice-cold water

1 Preheat the oven to 220°C (200°C fan/425°F/Gas 7). Line a large baking tray with baking parchment. Place the sweet potato, cut-side down, on the tray. Bake for 30 minutes or until tender. Allow to stand for 5 minutes to cool slightly.

2 Meanwhile, to make the wholemeal pie crust, process the hazelnut meal, rolled oats, flour, coconut oil, and a pinch of salt until fine crumbs form. With the motor operating, gradually add the 1/3 cup (80ml) ice-cold water until just combined. Press the mixture into an 18cm (1-litre) round pie tin. Refrigerate for 15 minutes or until chilled. Line the pastry with baking parchment; fill with dried beans or rice. Bake blind for 15 minutes. Remove the paper and beans; bake for a further 5 minutes or until the pastry is crisp.

3 When the sweet potatoes are cool enough to handle, scoop the flesh into the bowl of a food processor. Add the eggs, cooled melted chocolate, honey, flour, coconut milk, and vanilla; process until smooth and combined. Pour the mixture into the baked pie crust.

4 Reduce the oven temperature to 180°C (160°C fan/350°F/Gas 4). Bake the pie for 40 minutes or until just set. Allow to stand for 10 minutes, then refrigerate until chilled.

5 Dust the pie with the cocoa powder and serve with the coconut yogurt.

TIP

Dutch-process cocoa powder is darker than natural cocoa powder and has a mellower flavour. It goes through an alkalizing process when it is made, neutralizing the natural acidity of the cocoa beans.

Spiced date, ginger, and hazelnut pear cake

HEALTHY FATS/HIGH-FIBRE | PREP + COOK TIME **1 HOUR** | SERVES **10**
PER SERVING | Energy kcals 321 | Carbohydrate 37g of which sugar 23g | Fat 15g of which saturates 2g | Salt 0.6g | Fibre 4g

It is a myth that cooking with extra virgin olive oil destroys its benefits. Good-quality
extra virgin olive oil has a high smoke point of around 210°C, so it can be used for stir-fries,
frying, roasting, and baking without degrading. Store your oil in a cool, dark place to retain
the freshness and health-promoting properties.

$^3/_4$ cup (105g) hazelnuts

18 soft fresh dates (360g), pitted, halved

1 tsp bicarbonate of soda

$^1/_3$ cup (80ml) extra virgin olive oil, plus extra
for greasing

4 eggs

1$^1/_4$ cups (200g) wholemeal self-raising flour

2 tsp ground ginger

$^1/_3$ cup (80ml) pure maple syrup

3 ripe Packham pears (690g)

1 Preheat the oven to 180°C (160°C fan/350°F/Gas 4). Lightly grease a
23cm springform cake tin; double-line the bottom and side with baking
parchment. Process the hazelnuts to a fine flour-like texture. Set aside.

2 Put the dates, bicarbonate of soda, and $^1/_2$ cup (125ml) boiling water
in a large heatproof bowl; allow to stand for 5 minutes to soften. Process
the mixture until smooth.

3 Put the date mixture, ground hazelnuts, olive oil, eggs, flour, ginger,
and $^1/_4$ cup of the maple syrup in a large bowl; mix until just combined.
Peel and grate 1 of the pears; fold through the cake mixture.

4 Spoon the mixture into the prepared tin. Slice the remaining pears thinly.
Arrange the pear slices on top of the cake. Brush with the remaining
maple syrup.

5 Bake the cake for 50 minutes or until a skewer inserted into the centre
comes out clean. Leave the cake to stand in the pan for 10 minutes
before transferring to a wire rack to cool.

Easy fruit salads

Fruit salad may be simple to make, but you can enjoy an almost endless array of taste sensations by choosing complementary combinations ranging from the classic to the exotic. Just be sure to select good-quality, perfectly ripe fruit for the best results.

Orange and rosemary

PREP + COOK TIME **15 MINUTES** | SERVES **4**

Remove the zest from 1 orange in long, thin strips using a zesting tool; reserve the zest and the orange. Carefully peel 5 more oranges, discarding any pith. Cut all the oranges crossways into rounds. Combine the reserved zest strips, 1 cup (220g) caster sugar, $\frac{1}{2}$ cup (125ml) water, and 2 small sprigs of rosemary in a large microwave-safe bowl; microwave on HIGH (100%) for $2\frac{1}{2}$ minutes or until the sugar dissolves and the syrup is hot. Carefully add the orange slices and 2 tablespoons lemon juice. Allow to cool for 10 minutes. Serve the fruit salad topped with 2 tablespoons crumbled pistachio halva and $\frac{1}{2}$ cup pomegranate seeds. (Tip: Halva is a confection made from sesame seeds and sugar, and is available from Middle Eastern grocers and in some supermarkets.)

Watermelon and lychee

PREP + COOK TIME **20 MINUTES** | SERVES **8**

Cut 1.5kg seedless watermelon into batons. Peel and seed 16 fresh lychees. Put in a large bowl with 150g raspberries. Put $1\frac{1}{2}$ cups (330g) caster sugar and $1\frac{1}{2}$ cups (375ml) water in a medium microwave-safe bowl; microwave on HIGH (100%) for 3 minutes or until the sugar dissolves and the syrup is hot. Carefully remove the bowl from the microwave; add $\frac{1}{4}$ cup (60ml) lime juice, 2 teaspoons finely grated lime zest, and 1 teaspoon vanilla extract. Cool the syrup mixture by stirring over a bowl of iced water. Pour the syrup mixture over the fruit. Serve topped with extra lime zest.

Cherry and kombucha

PREP + COOK TIME **20 MINUTES** | SERVES **4**

Remove the stones from 225g fresh cherries; put the cherries in a large microwave-safe bowl with 1 cup (250ml) lemon and ginger kombucha. Microwave on HIGH (100%) for 2 minutes or until the cherries soften slightly, mashing the fruit slightly with a fork halfway through the cooking time. Stir in 2 teaspoons rosewater. Slice 500g strawberries into rounds; add to the cherry mixture with $1\frac{1}{2}$ teaspoons grated lemon zest. Spoon the fruit salad into 4 small serving bowls or 1-cup (250ml) dessert glasses; pour an extra $\frac{2}{3}$ cup (160ml) kombucha among the bowls. Serve immediately topped with lemon slices.

Mango and makrut

PREP + COOK TIME **20 MINUTES** | SERVES **4**

Remove the cheeks from 4 chilled mangoes. Using a large spoon, scoop to remove the mango cheek flesh in one piece. Cut the cheek flesh lengthways into slices; place in a large bowl. Grate 125g palm sugar into a small microwave-safe bowl; add $\frac{1}{2}$ cup (125ml) water and 6 shredded fresh makrut lime leaves. Microwave on HIGH (100%) for $1\frac{1}{2}$ minutes or until the sugar dissolves. Add 1 teaspoon finely grated lime zest and $\frac{1}{4}$ cup (60ml) lime juice. Pour the hot syrup over the mango; toss to combine. Serve the fruit salad topped with $\frac{1}{2}$ cup (30g) fresh or toasted flaked coconut.

Stone fruit sponge pudding

HIGH-FIBRE | PREP + COOK TIME **1 HOUR 10 MINUTES** | SERVES **4**
PER SERVING | Energy kcals 402 | Carbohydrate 40g of which sugar 29g | Fat 20g of which saturates 6g | Salt 0.3g | Fibre 4g

By using a variety of stone fruit for this pudding, you will benefit from the unique properties of each fruit type. With the plums, try to choose those that are also red-fleshed because they will contain more anthocyanins, plant pigments with high antioxidant activity that are of benefit to our immune system.

2 yellow nectarines (340g)

2 white peaches (300g)

2 small plums (150g)

$\frac{1}{4}$ cup (60ml) pure maple syrup

$\frac{1}{2}$ tsp ground cinnamon

3 eggs

1 tbsp light soft brown sugar

2 tsp finely grated lemon zest

1 tsp vanilla extract

2 tbsp white spelt flour

3 tsp cornflour

$\frac{1}{3}$ cup (40g) almond meal

30g butter, melted, cooled

2 tbsp flaked natural almonds

sifted icing sugar, to serve (optional)

1 Preheat the oven to 180°C (160°C fan/350°F/Gas 4). Lightly grease a 1.5-litre (6-cup) shallow oval ovenproof dish.

2 Halve the fruit; remove the stones. Cut the flesh into quarters. Put in a large bowl with the maple syrup and cinnamon; toss to combine. Add to the ovenproof dish. Cover with foil and bake for 25 minutes or until the fruit starts to soften.

3 Meanwhile, whisk together the eggs, brown sugar, lemon zest, and vanilla in the medium bowl of an electric mixer, on high, for 5 minutes or until ribbons form when the beaters are lifted. Sift the combined flours over the egg mixture, then add the almond meal and cooled butter. Using a large metal spoon, incorporate the ingredients gently. (Be careful not to overmix.)

4 Remove the foil from the ovenproof dish. Spoon the mixture evenly over the fruit; sprinkle with the flaked almonds. Bake the pudding for 18 minutes or until lightly golden. Lightly dust with sifted icing sugar to serve, if you like.

TIP

You could use four 1$\frac{1}{4}$-cup (310ml) ovenproof dishes to make individual puddings, if you like.

Honey and pineapple granita with coconut yogurt

FAST | PREP + COOK TIME **15 MINUTES + FREEZING** | SERVES **4**

PER SERVING | Energy kcals 331 | Carbohydrate 46g of which sugar 46g | Fat 13g of which saturates 9g | Salt 0.1g | Fibre 6g

Even the zest of lime has health benefits. The skin of citrus fruit contains the two antioxidants limonene and coumarin, which have been shown to stimulate a detoxification enzyme that in turn helps to rid the body of potentially carcinogenic compounds.

1 ripe pineapple (1.25kg)

2 limes (130g)

2 tbsp runny honey

1 cup (280g) dairy-free coconut yogurt

$\frac{1}{2}$ cup (25g) flaked coconut, toasted

1. Trim the pineapple, discarding the top, base, and skin. Cut in half lengthways; coarsely chop the flesh, including the core. You will need 650g pineapple flesh.

2. Finely grate the zest from 1 of the limes, then juice. Process the pineapple, honey, 2 tablespoons lime juice, and 2 teaspoons lime zest until smooth.

3. Strain the mixture into a jug, pressing down firmly to extract all the juice. Pour the juice into a 20cm x 30cm shallow rectangular baking tin. Freeze the granita mixture for 2½ hours or until firm.

4. Using a metal fork, break up any ice crystals in the tin; return the granita to the freezer. Repeat the process every hour for 2 more hours or until the granita is the texture of snow.

5. Divide the coconut yogurt among 4 serving glasses; top evenly with the granita. Thinly slice the remaining lime; top the granita with the lime and toasted flaked coconut. Serve immediately.

TIP

If your pineapple is not overly sweet, you may need to add a little extra honey, to taste.

Polenta and ricotta cake with rosemary lemon syrup

GLUTEN-FREE | PREP + COOK TIME **50 MINUTES** | SERVES **10**

PER SERVING | Energy kcals 362 | Carbohydrate 32g of which sugar 24g | Fat 21g of which saturates 5g | Salt 0.9g | Fibre 0g

Best made on the day of serving, this cake has a rich, yellow colour and an appealing crumbly texture courtesy of the polenta. And with polenta and almond meal replacing any wheat flour, it is a gluten-free option that sacrifices nothing when it comes to lemony zestiness.

2 lemons (280g)

$^3/_4$ cup (180g) fresh ricotta

$^1/_2$ cup (175g) runny honey

$^1/_3$ cup (80ml) extra virgin olive oil, plus extra for greasing

1 tsp vanilla bean paste

4 eggs, separated

$^2/_3$ cup (110g) instant polenta

1$^1/_4$ cups (150g) almond meal

2 tsp gluten-free baking powder

pinch of salt

rosemary lemon syrup

$^1/_3$ cup (115g) runny honey

4 large sprigs of rosemary

$^1/_4$ cup (60ml) lemon juice

1 tsp vanilla bean paste

2 small lemons (130g), thinly sliced into rounds

whipped lemon ricotta

$^3/_4$ cup (180g) reduced-fat fresh firm ricotta

1 tsp runny honey

1 tbsp lemon juice

TIP

Set the cake tin on a tray or baking sheet before pouring over the syrup, to catch any drips.

1 Put the lemons in a saucepan; cover with water, and bring to the boil. Top the lemons with a lid or small plate to keep submerged. Reduce the heat to medium, and simmer for 30 minutes or until tender. Drain. When the lemons are cool enough to handle, tear open; discard any pips.

2 Preheat the oven to 160°C (140°C fan/325°F/Gas 3). Lightly grease a 23cm springform tin; double-line the bottom and side with baking parchment.

3 Blend or process the lemons, ricotta, honey, olive oil, vanilla bean paste, and egg yolks until smooth.

4 Combine the polenta, almond meal, and baking powder in a large bowl; stir in the lemon mixture. Whisk the egg whites and a pinch of salt using an electric mixer until soft peaks form; fold through the polenta mixture. Spoon into the prepared tin, and smooth the top.

5 Bake the cake in the oven for 50 minutes or until a skewer inserted into the centre comes out clean.

6 Meanwhile, make the rosemary lemon syrup and whipped lemon ricotta. For the syrup, put the honey, $^1/_2$ cup (125ml) water, and rosemary sprigs in a small saucepan over a high heat. Bring to the boil; cook for 4 minutes. Add the lemon juice, vanilla, and lemon slices; simmer for 2 minutes. For the whipped lemon ricotta, blend or process the ricotta, honey, lemon juice, and 2 tablespoons water until smooth. Refrigerate until needed.

7 Spoon half of the hot rosemary lemon syrup over the warm cake while still in the tin; leave to stand until cooled. Transfer the cake to a plate, and serve with the remaining syrup and the whipped lemon ricotta.

Real chocolate crackles

FAST | PREP + COOK TIME **20 MINUTES + REFRIGERATION** | MAKES **10**
PER SERVING | Energy kcals 220 | Carbohydrate 24g of which sugar 10g | Fat 12g of which saturates 9g | Salt 0g | Fibre 3g

It's not just your imagination. Chocolate really can cheer you up! The carbohydrates present raise levels of serotonin, the feel-good chemical in your brain, and chocolate contains phenylethylamine, which acts as a mood elevator.

2 cups (30g) puffed brown rice

³/₄ cup (130g) raw buckwheat

1 cup (75g) shredded coconut

100g dark chocolate (85% cocoa), broken into chunks

¹/₄ cup (55g) coconut oil

2 tbsp runny honey

2 tbsp white chia seeds

15g packet freeze-dried strawberries, crushed

1 Preheat the oven to 180°C (160°C fan/350°F/Gas 4). Line ten holes of a 12-hole ¹/₃-cup (80ml) standard muffin tin with paper cases.

2 Spread the puffed rice and buckwheat over a large baking tray; bake for 4 minutes. Stir through the coconut; bake for a further 5 minutes or until evenly toasted. Allow to cool to room temperature.

3 Meanwhile, put the chocolate, coconut oil, and honey in a medium saucepan; stir over a low heat until melted and smooth.

4 Add the toasted dry ingredients and chia seeds to the chocolate mixture; stir to coat evenly. Spoon the mixture into the prepared paper cases. Sprinkle with the freeze-dried strawberries. Refrigerate the crackles for 30 minutes or until set.

TIP

Store these chocolate crackles in the refrigerator for up to 3 days. If you want to make 24 smaller chocolate crackles, set them in mini muffin cases.

Mango and raspberry friand tray bake

DAIRY-FREE | PREP + COOK TIME **50 MINUTES** | SERVES **12**

PER SERVING | Energy kcals 311 | Carbohydrate 18g of which sugar 12g | Fat 22g of which saturates 3g | Salt 0.1g | Fibre 2g

Inspiration for this recipe comes from friands, buttery little almond cakes similar to financiers. For ease we've made one large cake and reworked the recipe with olive oil replacing the traditional butter, and replaced and reduced the sugar by using maple syrup.

2 ripe mangoes (600g)

1/3 cup (80ml) extra virgin olive oil

1/3 cup (80ml) pure maple syrup, plus extra, to serve (optional)

4 eggs, separated

2 tsp vanilla bean paste

2 cups (240g) almond meal

1/2 cup (75g) white spelt flour

1 tsp ground cinnamon

1/2 tsp baking powder

125g raspberries

1/3 cup (40g) natural flaked almonds

1 Preheat the oven to 180°C (160°C fan/350°F/Gas 4). Line an 18cm x 27cm rectangular baking tin with baking parchment.

2 Cut the cheeks from the mango; peel. Cut the flesh from around the stone and one cheek to make 1 1/4 cups of firmly packed finely chopped mango. Slice the remaining mango cheek thinly; reserve.

3 Process the chopped mango with the olive oil, the 1/3 cup (80ml) maple syrup, egg yolks, and vanilla bean paste until completely smooth.

4 Sift the almond meal, flour, cinnamon, and baking powder into a large bowl, tipping any bran material left in the sieve back into the bowl as well. Stir through the mango mixture until half combined.

5 Beat the egg whites and a pinch of salt in a large clean bowl with an electric mixer until soft peaks form. Fold the egg white through the mango mixture until no lumps remain. (Be careful not to overmix.) Pour the mixture into the prepared tin. Carefully smooth the surface of the mixture; top with the reserved sliced mango and half of the raspberries.

6 Bake for 35 minutes or until puffed and golden, and when a skewer inserted into the centre of the cake comes out clean. Allow to cool in the tin.

7 Serve the friand tray bake topped with the remaining raspberries, flaked almonds, and extra maple syrup, if you like.

Conversion chart

A note on Australian measures

- One Australian metric measuring cup holds approximately 250ml.

- One Australian metric tablespoon holds 20ml.

- One Australian metric teaspoon holds 5ml.

- The difference between one country's measuring cups and another's is within a two- or three-teaspoon variance, and should not affect your cooking results.

- North America, New Zealand, and the United Kingdom use a 15ml tablespoon.

Using measures in this book

- All cup and spoon measurements are level.

- The most accurate way of measuring dry ingredients is to weigh them.

- When measuring liquids, use a clear glass or plastic jug with metric markings.

- We use large eggs with an average weight of 60g. Fruit and vegetables are assumed to be medium unless otherwise stated.

Dry measures

metric	imperial
15g	$^1/_2$oz
30g	1oz
60g	2oz
90g	3oz
125g	4oz ($^1/_4$lb)
155g	5oz
185g	6oz
220g	7oz
250g	8oz ($^1/_2$lb)
280g	9oz
315g	10oz
345g	11oz
375g	12oz ($^3/_4$lb)
410g	13oz
440g	14oz
470g	15oz
500g	16oz (1lb)
750g	24oz (1$^1/_2$lb)
1kg	32oz (2lb)

Liquid measures

metric	imperial
30ml	1 fluid oz
60ml	2 fluid oz
100ml	3 fluid oz
125ml	4 fluid oz
150ml	5 fluid oz
190ml	6 fluid oz
250ml	8 fluid oz
300ml	10 fluid oz
500ml	16 fluid oz
600ml	20 fluid oz
1000ml (1 litre)	1$^3/_4$ pints

Length measures

metric	imperial
3mm	$^1/_8$in
6mm	$^1/_4$in
1cm	$^1/_2$in
2cm	$^3/_4$in
2.5cm	1in
5cm	2in
6cm	2$^1/_2$in
8cm	3in
10cm	4in
13cm	5in
15cm	6in
18cm	7in
20cm	8in
22cm	9in
25cm	10in
28cm	11in
30cm	12in (1ft)

Oven temperatures

The oven temperatures in this book are for conventional ovens; if you have a fan-forced oven, decrease the temperature by 10–20 degrees.

	°C (Celsius)	°F (Fahrenheit)
Very slow	120	250
Slow	150	300
Moderately slow	160	325
Moderate	180	350
Moderately hot	200	400
Hot	220	425
Very hot	240	475

Index

Acknowledgments

DK would like to thank Sophia Young, Joe Reville,
Amanda Chebatte, and Georgia Moore for their
assistance in making this book.

The Australian Women's Weekly Test Kitchen in
Sydney has developed, tested, and photographed
the recipes in this book.